PENGUIN BOO

The

THE
CLOUDED
MIRROR

L. T. C.
Rolt

English Journeys

PENGUIN BOOKS

Published by the Penguin Group
Penguin Books Ltd, 80 Strand, London WC2R 0RL, England
Penguin Group (USA) Inc., 375 Hudson Street, New York, New York 10014, USA
Penguin Group (Canada), 90 Eglinton Avenue East, Suite 700, Toronto, Ontario, Canada M4P 2Y3
(a division of Pearson Penguin Canada Inc.)
Penguin Ireland, 25 St Stephen's Green, Dublin 2, Ireland
(a division of Penguin Books Ltd)
Penguin Group (Australia), 250 Camberwell Road, Camberwell, Victoria 3124, Australia
(a division of Pearson Australia Group Pty Ltd)
Penguin Books India Pvt Ltd, 11 Community Centre, Panchsheel Park, New Delhi – 110 017, India
Penguin Group (NZ), 67 Apollo Drive, Rosedale, North Shore 0632, New Zealand
(a division of Pearson New Zealand Ltd)
Penguin Books (South Africa) (Pty) Ltd, 24 Sturdee Avenue, Rosebank, Johannesburg 2196, South Africa

Penguin Books Ltd, Registered Offices: 80 Strand, London WC2R 0RL, England

www.penguin.com

'The Clouded Mirror' first published in *The Clouded Mirror* by J. Lane 1955
'Kilvert's Country' extracted from *Landscape with Machines* first published by Longman 1971
'Canal Crusade' extracted from *Landscape with Canals* first published by Allen Lane 1977
This selection published in Penguin Books 2009

3

All rights reserved

Set by Rowland Phototypesetting Ltd, Bury St Edmunds, Suffolk
Printed in England by Clays Ltd, St Ives plc

ISBN: 978-0-141-19103-4

www.greenpenguin.co.uk

Penguin Books is committed to a sustainable future
for our business, our readers and our planet.
The book in your hands is made from paper
certified by the Forest Stewardship Council.

Mixed Sources
Product group from well-managed
forests and other controlled sources
www.fsc.org Cert no. SA-COC-1592
© 1996 Forest Stewardship Council
FSC

Contents

The Clouded Mirror

From the heights of Malvern, or from the rim of the
northern Cotswolds, there can be seen in clear weather
a long ridge of mountain on the western horizon. It is
to be seen at its best on some bright evening after storm
when the air has the clarity and freshness of spring water.
Then this far off mountain looks as dark as midnight
against the sunset brightness. But though it appears then
so clearly it does not lose its mystery. It could be a bank
of gathering storm clouds or the rising curtain of night
itself so remote does it seem in its wildness from the lush
pastoral beauties and the gentle hills of the populous
Severn country. Visually, the most distant hill-top is the
edge of the world so that it is always easy to invest it
with a mystery which it does not in fact possess. In the
alchemy of distance, of storm or sunset light or summer
haze it becomes Hy Brasil or Hesperides, a land of saints
or of the ever youthful; a peak of lost Atlantis where live
a people simpler but wiser than we are. Perhaps such
hills should not be visited. Yet in this case it is not only
the distance which lends the enchantment. Even at close
quarters there is still magic in this mountain.

Travel west or south-west from Hereford through the
little hills and the gently swelling folds of this most
gracious and fruitful shire. Everywhere there is colour
and richness; richness of tall trees and great apple

orchards; of red fields misted with the green of springing corn or of wheat yellowing to harvest; of deep pastures populous with sleek, slow-moving Hereford cattle. The ample farms with their serried stack yards and spreading buildings of timber framing, brick and tile, rest easily in the midst of so bountiful a landscape. Since Saxon times this has been a country of prosperous and settled agriculture, and to this day no part of England seems more reassuring in its traditional stability or conveys more surely the promise of continuing fruitfulness. Yet we are no longer in middle England now but on the western marches. Suddenly, from some modest vantage point the land falls away and there before us stretches the same ridge of mountain. No landscape contrast could be more dramatic. No longer remote, it now marches across the whole western horizon to form the boundary wall of this gracious English park. And what a mighty wall it is; ten miles long, two thousand feet high and so precipitous that in all its length only two rough paths climb at breakneck gradients diagonally across its sheer escarpment. This, the eastern rampart of the Black Mountains, is fittingly called the Black Daren for, except when it catches the sunlight of early morning, its forbidding face lies always in so deep a shadow that no detail of rock or scree can be seen. Thus even from this immediate vantage no less than from the distant height of Cotswold this mountain still jealously holds its secret, brooding over the sunlit fields like a thundercloud which enhances their greenness by its own darkness.

Nowhere else does the lilting pastoral of rural England come to so sudden and so dramatic a full-stop. Northwards along the border the once disputed lands of Saxon and Celt intermingle among a maze of foothills, but here there is no such gentle transition. In all its untamed grandeur the old mountain kingdom of the Celt rears itself with the sudden menace of a great breaker in a calm sea. Its crest might still be the rim of the world. What undiscovered country lies upon the other side; what magic of Merlin or Glendower? Do Arthur and his knights lie sleeping there? Caerleon is not far off. Or is it peopled by the older, wilder, stranger spirits of the Mabinogion: false Blodeuedd, daughter of flowers, Gwydion the magician, and those Princes who are half gods, half men? Looking at that high, dark skyline it is easy to let the imagination run riot. The Romans, the Saxons, the Normans from their border watch towers, they also looked towards that threatening ridge but with a very real concern, for their interest in what might be taking place upon the other side was a highly practical one. The Black Mountains were once an eyrie of the Silures, a tribe who offered so stubborn a resistance to the legions that they were not so much subjected as contained by Rome. This was the border of the Roman world and the great fortress of Isca which we now call Caerleon has the same significance as the Norman keeps of Longtown or Tretower which threatened the no less troublesome descendants of the Silures.

South of this long, unbroken eastern wall there is a single outlier. This solitary mountain, standing quite apart like a sentinel guarding the gate of a kingdom, rises sheer from the vale to riven peak and ridge which look razor sharp. This is Skirrid Fawr, but it is also called the

Holy Mountain because men say that upon the instant of the crucifixion its rocky summit was torn apart like the veil of the temple. With this significant exception the Black Mountains consist of a great rectangle of highlands whose northern escarpment overlooks the valley of the Wye and which is bounded on the west by the Afon Llynfi, flowing north out of Llangorse lake, and on the south by the lovely valley of the Usk. The eastern wall is the first of five parallel mountain ridges which enclose between them four deep valleys. The easternmost and longest of these, the valley of the Honddu, is called the Vale of Ewyas. The other three are known simply by the names of the streams which water them: Grwyne Fawr, Grwyne Fechan and Rhian-Goll. These three are all tributaries of the Usk, but the Honddu turns northward when it leaves its valley and joins the Monnow which flows into the Wye at Monmouth. The valley of the Rhian-Goll is broad and dotted with many farms. The road from Abergavenny to Talgarth follows it and crosses the northern escarpment at a height of little more than a thousand feet. The other narrower and much wilder valleys have no such easy outlet, for this northern ridge rides higher towards the east and can be crossed only by steep trackways impassable in winter except on foot.

So much for the geography of these Black Mountains. Today no wild Silurians lurk in the secret valleys or have their eyries on the windy uplands. Arthur sleeps sound and Glendower is dead yet still this country casts a more potent spell than any Merlin or Gwydion could command and it is not to be prescribed or captured by any beating of topographical boundaries. I have known this ever since I lived as a small child above the valley of the Wye where the great rounded gables of the mountains' northern face, sweeping with so majestic a stoop and curve from highland to lowland, seemed indeed to be the end of my world. They were the magnet of my eyes and I knew them in every kind of weather; cold and impersonal as death in the white of winter snow; sharp in stormlight; lost in a curtain of cloud whose ragged hem swirled and eddied, lifted and fell again over the rain-dark screes; or hazily blue in the summer heats of whinberry time.

The old two-horse waggonette which first carried me over the edge of the world was a fairy chariot. One hot summer's day we plodded slowly across the wide moorland plateau below the peak of Pen-y-Beacon, laboured up the last long ascent to the high Bwlch-yr-Effengel (The Gospel Pass), and then dropped down, down, down into the Vale of Ewyas, to the ruined monastery of Ignatius at Capel-y-Ffyn and then on under the arching hazels of the highbanked lanes to the ruins of that much older priory of Llanthony. How entrancing was that first glimpse of this hitherto undiscovered country! The mind of the child is always captivated by the idea of hidden beauty or lost riches. He dreams that he may discover some forsaken garden or a cave filled with rare treasure. Perhaps it is that he is born with sense of the loss of Eden. Some lose that sense and search no more for their secret gardens, but for others it can become a quest for the Grail. I think it was the unexpected richness of the Vale of Ewyas which so enthralled me. I had thought to find a desolate table-land or to view another broad valley like that of the Wye, and instead I found these sombre mountains harbouring deep in their heart like an emerald this small world. It was a world full of colour and of fragrance, of sheltered, drowsy warmth, of the hum of insects and the bleat of distant sheep and of the sound of rushing water where the Honddu fell from leaf-dappled sunlight into cool shade.

As I learned later, the soil of the Vale of Ewyas belongs to the same kindly old red sandstone formation that has made the broader acres of Herefordshire so munificent. And in a setting which the mountains shelter so jealously, this red soil is a most generous nurse to all wild flowers. They bloom in unexcelled profusion. Never have I gathered richer harvests of wild strawberries than from these hedge banks, nor seen pastures so starred with orchids or autumn crocus in their season as those beside the Honddu. It was no wonder that the Austin Canons should build their Priory at Llanthony; that Walter Savage Landor should dream of creating there an earthly paradise and Ignatius Lyne of founding a new monastic order. But men often succeed in destroying what they most would cherish and here they have been given no opportunity to do so. This country is very old and very jealous of its secrets. It gives only to those of great understanding and it sent these intruders back by the way they came. The Priory of Llanthony became a ruin long before the dissolution and now the nineteenth-century church of Ignatius has crumbled likewise. As for Landor's earthly paradise it was never more than bare and roofless walls upon the mountainside above the old priory. Only the ancient, rigorous life of the small farmers

6

goes on. They are part of the valley, these successors of the Silures, accepting and accepted. They ask no favours from the country and are not disappointed; they are givers and not takers. They are no dreamers of dreams and yet the spell of the country holds them the more surely as Landor found to his cost when they pulled up his incongruous cypress trees faster than his Italian workmen could plant them and he retired defeated like his predecessors.

How much are we influenced in later life by the natural environment of our childhood? Does so deep and mysterious a country, seen through the eyes of childhood, affect the man? I know that it moved me deeply as a child, that I felt its loss profoundly, and that whenever I have come back to it I have found the same sense of wonder return unimpaired. Imagine then my interest when, a few years ago, I began to read Arthur Machen's autobiography *Far off Things* and came upon the following passage which seemed to echo my own thought:

'I shall always esteem it as the greatest piece of fortune that has fallen to me, that I was born in that noble, fallen Caerleon-on-Usk, in the heart of Gwent. My greatest fortune, I mean, from that point of view which I now more especially have in mind, the career of letters. For the older I grow the more firmly am I convinced that anything which I may have accomplished in literature is due to the fact that when my eyes were first opened in earliest childhood they had before them the vision of an enchanted land. As soon as I saw anything I saw Twyn Barlwym, that mystic tumulus, the memorial of peoples that dwelt in that region before the Celts left the Land of Summer. This guarded the southern limit of the great mountain wall in the west; a little northward was Mynydd Maen – the Mountain of the Stone – a giant, rounded billow; and still to the north mountains, and on fair, clear days one could see the pointed summit of the Holy Mountain by Abergavenny. It would shine, I remember, a pure blue in the far sunshine: it was a mountain peak in a fairy tale.'

Machen goes on to say how he envisaged, but never realised, a story which would recreate 'those vague impressions of wonder and awe and mystery that I myself received from the form and shape of the land of my boyhood and youth'. 'I mention it here,' he continues, 'chiefly because I would lay stress on my doctrine that in the world of imagination the child is indeed father of the man, that the man is nothing more than the child with an improved understanding certainly, with all sorts of technical advantages in the way of information and in the arts of expression, but, on the other hand, with the disadvantage of a dimmed imaginative eye and a weakened vision. There have been a few men who have kept the awe and the surmise of earlier years and have added to those miraculous gifts the acquired accomplishments of age and instruction; and these are the only men who are entitled to the name of genius.'

I agree with Machen. But I would go further and say that although everything when first seen by the eye of a child is a thing of wonder, that wonder is more readily lost if the environment is an overwhelmingly man-made one of bricks and mortar, pavements, macadam and roaring traffic. It is better by far to open our eyes upon fields and green trees, although even here there can be degrees of good fortune. I believe that some places can exercise a greater power over the spirit than others, and that Machen was indeed fortunate because this strange country of the Southern Marches is pre-eminently such a place.

Once when I was climbing the great wall of the Black Daren on my way from Longtown to Llanthony the clouds suddenly rolled down upon the mountain in a dense white blanket which beaded everything with moisture, cut off all sight and sound, and reduced my world to the few feet of path immediately ahead of me. When I had crossed the narrow ridge and begun the steep descent I stopped for a few moments in fascination at the sight of the mists, born upon ascending air currents, sweeping up the almost sheer face of the mountain out of the invisible valley below like steam from a cauldron. As I watched, the dead whiteness of the cloud gradually became golden, assumed a dazzling brightness, swirled, eddied and then dissolved like mist from a mirror. There below, basking in sunshine, lay the valley pastures, their greenness unbelievably brilliant and jewel-like in that sudden revelation. But after a few moments the vision was gone as quickly as it had come. Colour and light lost their lustre, faded and then disappeared to leave me lost in the same white blindness as before. I take this as an image because I believe that in this country there remains some mysterious warmth and that the mist upon the mirror of the world is not so dense here as it is elsewhere; that there are occasions when it will suddenly melt and dissolve to reveal for a moment to our dulled senses an unbearable brightness, a terrible beauty.

Certainly this country has been the nurse of men who fully justified Arthur Machen's definition of genius; men to whom that beauty was revealed because they did not lose the child's clear vision but treasured it, using their worldly experience and their learning humbly as a means of understanding. Such a one was Henry Vaughan. Vaughan was born at Newton by Usk near to the lake of Llangorse on the western fringe of the Black Mountains. He came of the old Welsh family of Vaughan of Tretower whose fortified manor house stands close beside the more ancient Norman tower in the valley of the Rhian-goll a few miles to the east. He and his twin brother Thomas were educated by Matthew Herbert who was rector of Llangattock, a village on the bank of the Usk opposite the little town of Crickhowell which looks northward towards the two massive shoulders, Table Mountain and Blaen yr hen Ban, at the mouth of the Grwyne Fechan valley. Thus Vaughan was very much a part of this country and indeed knew no other until, in 1638, it is believed that he left Newton to complete his studies in Oxford and London. After the failure of the Royalist cause which he actively supported, he returned to his native country where he remained for the rest of his long life. How deep was his attachment to his own place, how sensible he was of the debt which he owed to it and to his native blood is evident from the fact that he styled himself 'Henry Vaughan, Silurist' in memory of his ancient ancestors. Moreover he entitled his book of secular verse 'Olor Iscanus', 'The Swan of Usk', and set upon title page and verso the paraphrase from the Georgics of Virgil and which may be freely translated: 'Lost to fame, I love the streams and woodlands; oh let me be laid in the cool glades of Usk and covered in the immeasurable shade of branches.' But Vaughan's fame rests, not upon his 'Olor Iscanus' but upon 'Silex Scintillans,' his book of religious poems which, though first published a year earlier, was actually completed later.

Vaughan was much influenced by George Herbert, himself a child of the Welsh border, and, to a much lesser degree, by John Donne, yet he spoke with his own authentic voice, a voice as clear and as musical as the waters of the river he loved so much. In his greatest poems it was an inspired voice, soaring to heights not to be scaled again in English poetry until Blake's 'Songs of Innocence' appeared one hundred and fifty years later. The reader will look in vain in the poems of 'Silex Scintillans' for any descriptions of scenery or indeed for any specific references to the country which he loved. For he was not a 'nature poet' in the sense in which that term was later to be applied. That detached, self-conscious and often merely sentimental regard for natural beauty for its own sake belongs to a later day. Vaughan did not, as it were, stand apart from his world and look at it as an art critic looks at a picture. It was part of his being, and though it was his most precious possession he valued it not for itself alone but as the mirror of an eternal world. There are flowers in his poems, birds sing in them and they are murmurous with streams and showers, yet all these are for him those weaker glories which are but the shadows of eternity. His favourite images are those of light; his poems are so shot through with sunlight, moonlight and starlight that they shine with a dazzling whiteness more bright in purity than any earthly light. Dawn captivates him and he makes of the dayspring a most moving symbol in such lines as these:

> 'Early, while yet the dark was gay,
> And gilt with stars more trim than day,
> Heaven's Lily and the Earth's chaste Rose,
> The green, immortal Branch arose,
> And in a solitary place
> Bowed to His Father His blessed face.'

Even when he writes of night, the dark is filled with moon or starlight or luminous with some supernatural radiance as when, in what is, perhaps, his greatest poem, 'The Night', he refers to his God as 'a deep but dazzling darkness'.

One of his recurrent themes was that 'the great chime and symphony of nature', as he called it, was the reflection of the eternal and existed to praise its Creator. He saw man as a part of this creation uniquely endowed with the capacity to see its wonders and to render that praise but as having forfeited that endowment. He did not see man's loss of Eden as the immediate consequence of Adam's fall but rather as the result of a continuing process of estrangement, a gradual falling off and loss of vision. We were no longer, he thought, so near the heart of things as 'those first white pilgrims' or 'the youthful world's gray fathers' who:

> Did with intentive looks watch every hour
> For thy new light, and trembled at each shower.

This is in the poem in which he takes the rainbow as his symbol and in which he continues:

> When thou dost shine, Darkness looks white and fair,
> Forms turn to music, clouds to smiles and air:
> Rain gently spends his honey-drops, and pours
> Balm on the cleft earth, milk on grass and flowers.

Vaughan, two hundred and fifty years before Arthur Machen, expresses the same conviction that, in the world of imagination, the child is father to the man and that the imaginative eye closes with the years. But unlike Machen he uses this personal experience to symbolise the loss which he believes mankind as a whole has suffered in the lifetime of the race. In 'The Retreat' he writes:

> Happy those early dayes! when I
> Shin'd in my Angell-infancy.
> Before I understood this place
> Appointed for my second race,
> Or taught my soul to fancy ought
> But a white, Celestiall thought;
> When yet I had not walkt above
> A mile, or two, from my first love,
> And looking back (at that short space,)

Could see a glimpse of his bright face;
When on some gilded Cloud, or flowre
My gazing soul would dwell an houre,
And in those weaker glories spy
Some shadows of eternity;
Before I taught my tongue to wound
My Conscience with a sinfull sound,
Or had the black art to dispence
A sev'rall sinne to ev'ry sence
But felt through all this fleshly dresse
Bright shootes of everlastingnesse.
    O how I long to travell back
And tread again that ancient track!

But having once put on the adult burden of knowledge
and experience it is not easy to travel back as Vaughan
himself discovered. For the way is not to be found
amongst external things but within the self. That is his
message. In 'Vanity of Spirit' he writes:

'I summoned nature; pierced through all her store;
Broke up some seals, which none had touched before;
Her womb, her bosom, and her head,
Where all her secrets lay a-bed,
I rifled quite; and having past
Through all the creatures, came at last
To search myself, where I did find
Traces and sounds of a strange kind.'

In the opening poem of 'Olor Iscanus' Vaughan expressed a wish and a resolve and also a great love. He wrote:

'But Isca, whensoe'r those shades I see,
And thy lov'd Arbours must no more know me,
When I am layd to rest hard by thy streams,
And my sun sets, where first it sprang in beams,
I'le leave behind me such a large, kind light,
As shall redeem thee from oblivious night,
And in these vowes which (living yet) I pay
Shed such a Previous and Enduring Ray,
As shall from age to age thy fair name lead
Till rivers leave to run, and men to read.'

Certainly this great and good man fulfilled his resolve. He also obtained his wish. He sleeps at Llansantffraed where his brother was vicar for many years, not within the church as might be expected of a Vaughan, but under the skies close to his beloved Isca. A great stone, quarried near Cwm-du in the valley of the Rhian-goll, covers him. It bears his name: 'Henricus Vaughan, Siluris', the arms of Vaughan of Tretower, and an inscription characteristic in its simplicity and humility:

Quod in Sepulchrum
Voluit
Servus inutilis:
Peccator Maximus
Hic Jaceo
✛
Gloria Miserere

If, as Henry Vaughan believed, the spirits of poets linger in the places they have loved, then the spirit of the Silurist must surely walk upon these hills or beneath the green shades of Usk. For his light does not fade. He has, too, a worthy companion.

In 1895, a booklover named William Brookes discovered on a stall in the Farringdon Road two manuscript books of verse and prose which he believed to be the work of Henry Vaughan. He bought them for a few pence and resold them to a Doctor Alexander Grosart who shared his opinion and proposed including them in a new edition of Vaughan's works. Before he could do so, however, Grosart died and the manuscripts passed to the bookseller and bibliophile Bertram Dobell. Despite their similarities of thought, Dobell became convinced that these books did not speak with the voice of the Silurist. Who then was their author? It was their original discoverer, Brookes, who ultimately came upon the vital clue and thus completed one of the most romantic, fortuitous and important literary discoveries of all time. He found in the British Museum a small book of verse in which he detected certain striking correspondences. The book bore no author's name, but the preface stated that he was private chaplain to Sir Orlando Bridgman, Lord Keeper of the Seal to Charles II. Research proved that Sir Orlando's chaplain was a certain Thomas Traherne, known author of two published books, *Roman Forgeries* and *Christian Ethics*. In the latter book, Dobell found a passage of verse identical with one in the anonymous manuscripts, so their authorship was thus proved beyond doubt. In this way the finest work of Thomas Traherne appeared in print for the first time over two hundred years after his death. Dobell published the poems in 1903 and in 1908 gave to the world one of its truly great books, the prose passages of Traherne, which he entitled *Centuries of Meditations*.

By a combination of the findings of research with certain autobiographical references in the 'Meditations', the broad outline of Traherne's short life has been subsequently pieced together chiefly as a result of the labours of Miss Gladys Wade. Yet he remains a more shadowy and elusive figure than Vaughan. Even the date of his birth cannot be determined, though the year is believed to have been 1638. He was born in Hereford, the son of a shoemaker, and the years of his childhood saw the city become the victim of siege and counter-siege by Royalist and Roundhead. He came of Celtic stock, like Vaughan, and is thought to have been a kinsman of the Trahernes of Lugwardine, one of whom, Philip Traherne, was three times mayor of Hereford. It was most probably due to the patronage of this influential connection that he received so good an education. It is conjectured that he was privately tutored, probably somewhere in the country outside the city during the upheavals of the Civil War. The first certain fact in his life is that he was entered as a Commoner of Brasenose College, Oxford, on the first of March, 1653, and matriculated a month later. In 1656 he graduated, was ordained and returned to his native Herefordshire for about a year before he was appointed to the living of Credenhill in December, 1657. He then went back to Oxford where he devoted four more years to intensive study and obtained his M.A. degree. Only then did he take up his Credenhill appointment. It was six years later that he became chaplain to

Sir Orlando Bridgman and looked his last on his native county. He died in the autumn of 1674 at the age of thirty-six. We neither know the date of his death nor the place of his burial, although he is said to lie beneath the lectern of the church at Teddington whither Sir Orlando had retired when he fell from favour at Court.

These are the bare facts of the life of Thomas Traherne; a short life and obscure and one of little achievement measured in worldly terms. So it might have remained had not William Brookes discovered his true greatness upon that stall in the Farringdon Road two hundred years later and purchased it for a song.

The little village of Credenhill lies five miles west of Hereford on the southern slopes of a hill crowned by the remains of an Iron Age camp which was built, no doubt, to watch the troubled border. The square tower of the church of St Mary with its ancient jewelled glass looks out across the vale of the Wye and over the border foothills about the Golden Valley to that long dark skyline of the Black Daren. This is the prospect which Thomas Traherne must so often have contemplated during his six fruitful years as a country parson. It is fascinating to think that these two men, the middle-aged Silurist by his beloved Usk, the young parson in his Herefordshire rectory, both deeply influenced by the same country, both following the same mystical path and holding so much in common that the work of the one could be mistaken for that of the other, lived for six years upon opposite sides of these same mountains and yet remained quite unknown to each other.

That Traherne was profoundly influenced by this

country, that for him, as for Vaughan, it became the mirror of eternity, there can be no question. We have it upon his own authority in the third of the *Centuries of Meditations* which is the most frankly autobiographical of all his writing. First there was its influence upon his early childhood when, he says, 'All appeared new, and strange at first, inexpressibly rare and delightful and beautiful. I was a little stranger, which at my entrance into the world was saluted and surrounded with innumerable joys. My knowledge was divine. I knew by intuition those things which since my Apostasy, I collected again by the highest reason.' He follows this with an evocation of his childhood and of the child's sense of wonder which is not to be matched in the whole range of English literature, whether prose or poetry. It is, deservedly, the best known of all Traherne's work, but it cannot be quoted too often:

'The corn was orient and immortal wheat, which never should be reaped, nor was ever sown. I thought it had stood from everlasting to everlasting. The dust and stones of the street were as precious as gold: the gates were at first the end of the world. The green trees when I saw them first through one of the gates transported and ravished me, their sweetness and unusual beauty made my heart to leap, and almost mad with ecstacy, they were such strange and wonderful things. The Men! O what venerable and reverend creatures did the aged seem! Immortal Cherubims! And young men glittering and sparkling Angels, and maids strange seraphic pieces of life and beauty! Boys and girls tumbling in the street, and playing, were moving jewels. I knew not that they were born or should die; but all things abided eternally as they were in their proper places. Eternity was manifest in the light of the day, and something infinite behind everything appeared: which talked with my expectation and moved my desire. The city seemed to stand in Eden, or to be built in Heaven. The streets were mine, the temple was mine, the people were mine, their clothes and gold and silver were mine, as much as their sparkling eyes, fair skins and ruddy faces. The skies were mine, and so were the sun and moon and stars, and all the World was mine; and I the only spectator and enjoyer of it. I knew no churlish proprieties, nor bounds, nor divisions: but all proprieties and divisions were mine: all treasures and the possessors of them. So that with much ado I was corrupted, and made to learn the dirty devices of this world. Which now I unlearn, and become, as it were, a little child again that I may enter into the Kingdom of God.'

Traherne goes on to tell how 'The first Light which shined in my infancy in its primitive and innocent clarity was totally eclipsed; insomuch that I was fain to learn all again.' How was it eclipsed? 'By the customs and manners of men,' he answers, 'which like contrary winds blew it out: by an innumerable company of other objects, rude, vulgar and worthless things, that like so many loads of earth and dung did overwhelm and bury it: by the impetuous torrent of wrong desires in all others that I saw or knew that carried me away and alienated me from it: by a whole sea of other matters and concernments that covered and drowned it . . .' Of the other 'objects', the worthless things, he goes on to say: 'You would not think how these barbarous inventions spoil your knowledge. They put grubs and worms in men's heads that are enemies to all pure and true apprehensions, and eat out all their happiness. They make it impossible for them, in whom they reign, to believe there is any excellency in the Works of God, or to taste any sweetness in the nobility of nature, or to prize any common, though never so great a blessing. They alienate men from the life of God, and at last make them to live without God in the world.'

Having been with so much ado corrupted, how did this 'divine philosopher' unlearn and become, as he says, a little child again, but with the addition of such understanding as this? Through the medium of that orient and immortal wheat and those green trees which had so ravished him as a child. Two profound spiritual experiences opened the way and directed the course of his life and both occurred in his own country, the first shortly before he went up to Oxford for the first time, and the second either after his first return in 1657 or later at Credenhill. Upon the first occasion, which he describes in the poem 'Solitude' and in the 'Meditations', he found himself alone in a field in the half-light of an evening of storm. We cannot know where he was at the time, but it is likely that the long skyline of the Black Daren formed his western horizon. Dark and threatening indeed it must have looked in such a stormlight. Newly returned from the life of the town, 'the very silence did me grieve', he says in his poem. He experienced a sudden agony of desolation and of loss in which nothing about him could give him any solace or companionship:

'They silent stood;
Nor earth, nor woods, nor hills, nor brooks, nor skies,
Would tell me where the hidden good,
Which I did long for, lies:
The shady trees,
The evening dark, the humming bees,
The chirping birds, mute springs and fords, conspire,
While they deny to answer my Desire.'

And yet Vaughan's 'great chime and symphony of
nature' had a lesson for him as he relates in his prose
account of the same occasion: 'Another time in a lowering and sad evening, being alone in the field, when all
things were dead and quiet, a certain want and horror
fell upon me, beyond imagination. The unprofitableness
and silence of the place dissatisfied me; its wideness
terrified me; from the utmost ends of the earth fears
surrounded me. How did I know but dangers might
suddenly arise from the East, and invade me from the
unknown regions beyond the seas? I was a weak and
little child, and had forgotten there was a man alive in
the earth. Yet something also of hope and expectation
comforted me from every border. This taught me that
I was concerned in all the world: and that in the re-
motest borders the causes of peace delight me, and the
beauties of the earth when seen were made to entertain me: that I was made to hold communion with the
secrets of divine providence in all the world: that a
remembrance of all the joys I had from my birth ought
always to be with me.' He saw, in the words of another
Meditation, that 'all things were well in their proper

places; I alone was out of frame and had need to be mended.'

The result of the second spiritual experience which finally determined the course of his life can be described very simply in his own words: 'When I came into the country, and being seated among silent trees, and meads and hills, had all my time in mine own hands, I resolved to spend it all, whatever it cost me, in search of happiness, and to satiate that burning thirst which nature had enkindled in me from my youth.' The search for happiness; it sounds a selfish and unsatisfactory ambition. But happiness for Traherne did not mean, as it means to us, vicarious pleasure or amusement; it meant that felicity and certitude which comes from a combining of the child's clear eye of wonder with adult experience to produce true understanding. This, the most difficult of all achievements, was what Thomas Traherne accomplished in his short life. This was the measure of his greatness and it brought a great reward. It is doubtful whether any happier man has ever lived, and so concerned was he to communicate his experience and share his happiness, to show others the road he had followed, that exultation gushes from his pen like water from a spring.

It is in the *Centuries of Meditations*, with its measured cadences, its sustained periods and its haunting reiterations which chime like bells that Traherne's spring of joy finds its true voice. In verse he is less successful and is by no means so great a poet as Vaughan. Despite his use of natural imagery, the white radiance of Vaughan's greatest poems is of a quality no longer of this world.

One thinks of moonlight reflected in some cold, clear pool not flawed by any stir and fret of wind or current, and for such an unearthly tranquility his poetry is the natural medium. Compared with these still depths, Traherne's thought is as impetuous as a mountain torrent, gathering every runlet to itself, throwing up a spray shot through by sunlight with rainbow colours, singing with the ecstacy of its own life and movement and not to be contained between the banks of any metre or strict form. Yet Traherne's work, despite this impression of eager spontaneity, was, no less than that of the Silurist, the fruit of discipline, of learning, of high craftsmanship, and of complete singleness of mind and purpose.

Traherne was, in fact, a greater scholar than Vaughan. It would be quite wrong to suppose that his quest of felicity, his aim 'to become, as it were, a little child again', caused him to abandon reason, to neglect the powers of his intellect and the teachings of his forerunners. On the contrary he saw all these as means of understanding, as tools to serve his unswerving purpose. He studied widely, not only the early Christian masters, but those still earlier philosophers, especially Plato and Plotinus, whose teachings had influenced the development of Christian doctrine. The major of the two books published in his lifetime, *Roman Forgeries*, is a work of great research and scholarship and is of interest today simply because of the light it sheds upon the extent of Traherne's learning. The purpose of the book was to provide textual proof of the extent to which the Roman church had falsified the records of the early Christian councils in order to strengthen Papal power. Nevertheless, despite this book and despite the fact that he became a priest of the Anglican church, Traherne was no narrow sectarian. He took no part whatever in the bitter controversies which then raged between the Roman church, the Reformed church and the new Nonconformist sects. On the contrary he represented the one intellectual movement of the day which, had it proved strong enough to prevail, might have achieved a new Christendom and changed the course of history. For although he was not a Cambridge man he was the finest flower of that group of thinkers who are now referred to historically as the 'Cambridge Platonists'.

These men were most concerned to reaffirm the immanence of God at a time when religious thought was unduly preoccupied with transcendence; that is to say, with the concept of God without the world rather than that of God within. It is in fact no paradox that as a result of this preoccupation religious organisations had become more worldly and theology more involved in the historic and the temporal. Traherne proclaimed God within the soul of man and within the world as well as beyond the world. He was concerned to point out that path to truth which has guided all the great mystics of the world: first to discover the God within, then to see the God manifest in creation, and then to know that these are temporal aspects of the eternal. By following this path a point of certitude may be reached where it is no longer difficult to reconcile immanence with transcendence, but where it can be understood that an eternal being can exist within the heart of all created things and yet, despite their continuous becoming, remain eternally unchanged. In this regard, to become aware of God within the microcosm is simply to affirm his existence beyond the macrocosm. Hence reason becomes an instrument of understanding because the more we learn about our world the more assured and triumphant is the affirmation.

This was the difficult path Traherne followed with so much pains to the exultant conclusion which he proclaimed in the *Centuries*. Others had taken the same hard road before him but, like all profound truths, this, the very fountainhead of religious thought, needs recurrent re-affirmation in order that it may remain vital and undistorted. If it is not renewed by that eternal spring which Traherne divined, the flow of the river of religious thought grows sluggish and stagnates, its clear stream made obscure by the silt of ritual and of a theology which may be finely reasoned but which is no longer deeply felt. As symbolic acts and derived truths accumulate so there is the greater danger that these 'signs' will tend to be revered for themselves and that the reality of the thing signified will become obscured. Ultimately, such accumulations of silt settle in shoals which divide the river of religious thought into separate and irreconcilable channels. This is precisely what had occurred in seventeenth-century England. With the exception of the Cambridge Platonists, religious thought had become so obsessed with the trees that it had lost sight of the wood.

Differences of creed and ritual trivial by comparison with the great unifying truth proclaimed by Traherne had torn Christendom to pieces, so bitter and so profoundly unchristian were the hostilities which they provoked. These warring sects all shared to some extent a common error in that their orthodoxy had become overwhelmingly transcendental. For them God was without but no longer within the world and there was therefore a fundamental distinction between the transcendent truth revealed by religion and the truths discoverable by reason. Thus the tendency was to renounce the world and the flesh along with the devil and to fix the attention of the faithful upon a paradise hereafter as a reward for 'fighting the good fight' in what became known as 'the battle of life'. As a consequence of man's first fall, God had withdrawn from his creation to become the remote referee in the human struggle. Traherne did not fall into this fatal error. For him God was immanent in the world so that to condemn the world and to withdraw from it because of evils in the world for which man alone was responsible was tantamount to blasphemy. 'To contemn the world and to enjoy the world,' he declares, 'are things contrary to each other. How then can we contemn the world, which we are born to enjoy? Truly there are two worlds. One was made by God, the other by men. That made by God was great and beautiful. Before the Fall it was Adam's joy and the Temple of his Glory. That made by men is a Babel of Confusions: invented riches, pomps and vanities, brought in by sin . . . Leave the one that you may enjoy the other.' Unfortunately the orthodox religious thought of the time drew no such distinction but threw away the jewel along with the dross.

It was as a result of this unbalanced state of religious thought that men like Descartes and Hobbes could propound their desolate theories of the nature of the material universe and still profess an orthodox religious belief without any awareness of inconsistency. The momentous and tragic outcome of this fatal severance of the temporal from the eternal, the immanent from the transcendent, we now plainly see, and it was to heal this breach that Traherne and his fellows strove so hard but, as events have proved, so unsuccessfully. They saw the materialistic world picture of Descartes and Hobbes for the sad, Godless and evil thing it was. For Traherne the world was neither a vale of tears to be renounced, nor a mine of material riches, but the mirror of the eternal to be enjoyed in wonder. Reason was no enemy of belief, it was the instrument of understanding, of praise and of joy. To use Traherne's words, it was the function of reason 'to restore the pieces to their proper places . . . we being then Kings over the whole world, being perfectly pleased with the whole composure'. It was only when man's reason was arbitrarily sundered from vision and belief that it became the deadly nurse of pride, leading him headlong towards self-destruction and cutting him off forever from that Eden which Vaughan and Traherne saw all about them.

Although the dust of this 'divine philosopher' lies far from his beloved country, surely his rare spirit walks with the shade of the Silurist upon these border hills. For they travelled to the heart of things, these two, and so became themselves a part of this country's magic. 'Is it not a great thing,' asks Traherne, 'that you should be Heir of the World?' The cloud upon Skirrid Fawr becomes golden, lifts, and then dissolves like mist from a mirror to leave the riven peak of the mountain as clear and as blue as a sapphire in the sunlight. And then, ringing so clearly down the centuries, that great answer comes: 'It is the Paradise of God. It is more to man since he is fallen than it was before. It is the place of Angels and the Gate of Heaven.'

Kilvert's Country

An important literary event occurred in July 1938 when the *Diary* of Francis Kilvert was published. As most people now know, from 1865 to 1872 Kilvert was curate at Clyro, a Radnorshire village just across the Wye from Hay. As a result of the acclaim with which this *Diary* was rightly received, Kilvert has become a minor literary celebrity and there is even a Kilvert Society whose members make an annual pilgrimage to what is now often referred to as Kilvert's Country. Naturally, when we moved into the Hay district in the fateful summer of 1914 this was all in the future and, so far as I know, we never even heard the name of Kilvert mentioned. Although this simple, kindly man was evidently beloved in his parish, his short life would have ended in oblivion had he not shyly recorded, with no thought of publication, his great love for the people and the landscape of this part of the Welsh Border.

Kilvert was neither the first nor the last man to be influenced by the powerful magic of this mountain country. I know that in my early boyhood its beauty and wildness was capable of inducing in me a strange feeling of intense exaltation that was part awed reverence and part terror. It could make my spine tingle and the hair on my head stand up. It was from such experiences and not from the teachings of any organised religion that

there has stemmed my conviction that there is a God
beyond human conceptions of good and evil. The reverse
of this medal is that I believe these same experiences to
be the source of my lifelong interest in supernatural evil.
When, much later in life, I discovered the great mystical
writings of the Silurist Henry Vaughan and his contem-
porary Thomas Traherne, I realised with shock of wonderment that they had been similarly influenced by the
same landscape. And when, at about the same time, I
read those short stories of Arthur Machen, *The Novel of
the Black Seal*, *The Great God Pan*, *The Shining Pyramid*
and *The White People*, I knew that he, born at Caerleon,
had experienced its darker side. Yet Machen also has
expressed his belief 'that man is made a mystery for
mysteries and visions, for the realisation in his conscious-
ness of ineffable bliss, for a great joy that transmutes
the whole world, for a joy that surpasses all joys and
overcomes all sorrows'.

Although there are several references to Wordsworth
in his *Diary*, Kilvert never mentions Henry Vaughan,
while Machen was still unborn. As for Traherne, the
seventeenth-century incumbent of the nearby parish of
Credenhill, he, like Kilvert himself, enjoys a posthumous
fame, for his greatest work, *The Centuries of Meditations*,
was only discovered by chance in 1895, sixteen years after
Kilvert's untimely death at Bredwardine. Yet a single
terse and otherwise inexplicable sentence: 'An angel satyr
walks these hills', which suddenly appears in his *Diary*
between mundane trivialities under the date 20 June
1871 reveals that Kilvert, too, was of this company. But
whereas the ordinary mortal cannot exist for very long

on the mystical plane that Vaughan and Traherne inhabit, the great merit of Kilvert's *Diary* is that it is a faithful reflection of life itself in its rapid shifts from pathos to bathos, from the sublime to the ridiculous and from prose of visionary quality to homespun detail or country gossip. It is for this reason and also because no other book has the power to evoke such vivid memories of my childhood that his *Diary* has become one of my favourite bedside books.

In 1914, so little had changed in the district during the forty-four years that had passed since Kilvert wrote, that his world became my world, and by this I mean not only the landscape but the way of life of the folk who peopled it. The men and women I remember, riding their sure-footed ponies down from their lonely mountain farms to crowd the little streets of Hay on market days, were still such people as Kilvert knew and described so affec-tionately. Many of the local landowners and middle-class families bore the same names as they did in his day, and in summer they still joined forces in communal walks and picnics such as he describes. I took part in many of these neighbourly excursions. Even today, the district has changed less than anywhere else I know outside western Ireland.

Kilvert's *Diary* has its darker side. Reading it, one cannot but be aware that the writer was always acutely conscious of life's transience. It could scarcely have been otherwise when it fell to the lot of that sentimental and susceptible curate to read the burial service over many of those rosy country girls about whose charms he waxed so eloquent. Like so many early faded flowers, he would watch them sicken and die. Tuberculosis was then the arch enemy of youth and in 1914 the disease was still rife in the district, particularly in the mountain farms. Tombstones in the local churchyards reveal that the people either succumbed to this scourge before they were thirty or they lived to a ripe old age.

Kilvert's characteristic Victorian reticence and inhibition, not to say prurience, on the subject of sex was offset by a realistic attitude towards death which we now find morbid. We do so because our way of thinking on these subjects has turned topsy-turvy since Kilvert's day. Obsessively frank about sexual matters, we are extremely reticent about death as though trying to pretend it does not exist. This is misguided. So far from being morbid, a constant awareness that 'all flesh is grass' makes us appreciate the beauty of the world and the potential riches of life the more keenly. Kilvert's *Diary* is a proof of this. His love of natural beauty and his zest for the small, homely pleasures of life would not shine so brightly from his pages were it not for an awareness of life's brevity which he makes his readers share.

I learnt to appreciate this myself during my years at Hay, for I was then a sickly small boy who occasioned his parents considerable anxiety. I suffered from recurrent bouts of bronchitis which confined me to bed with a 'low fever' for weeks on end each winter. It was feared I had fallen a victim to the prevalent disease and there was dark whispered talk about a suspected 'patch' on my lungs. But my blood seemed to respond like sap to the lengthening days. Spring spelled convalescence and summer full health. Consequently I savoured these far off spring and summer days so intensely that memories of them now seem ineffably sweet.

I should like to be able to say that my home during these years was some romantic old house in the mountains, but the truth is far more prosaic. The architecture of every small town along the Welsh Marches reveals the fact that there was a sudden increase in their moneyed population in late Victorian or early Edwardian times bringing a brief period of prosperity. The more wealthy of these immigrants emparked land and built themselves considerable mansions, but the majority were content with neat detached villas surrounded by large gardens. This influx was reflected in the towns by the building of new shops, hotels and public buildings: market halls, town halls and clock towers. By contrast with the bleak and characterless cubes of today, many of these buildings have now acquired a certain period charm, but in 1914 we regarded them as hideously over ornate. No book that I have read about the Welsh Border even mentions this social phenomenon. I suspect the reason for it was that the belated coming of railways to the Marches made such small towns suddenly accessible. At a time when it was becoming more difficult and more expensive to lead the life of a country gentleman, railways opened up a new territory where property was cheap, where there was no shortage of domestic servants and where good fishing and rough shooting could be had for the asking. These were certainly the considerations that drew, first my uncle Harry and then my father to Hay.

In the scattered parish of Cusop, lying a little to the south of Hay, a small housing estate had been built at the turn of the century which was known locally as 'the Forty Acres'. The houses, which an agent would describe as 'desirable detached residences standing in own grounds', were served by a rectangle of narrow road that enclosed a single green field. This central field has since been built upon and there are other examples of what the planners call 'judicious infilling', but in 1914 there were, at most, a dozen houses and my father acquired one of the more retired of these. It was called 'Radnor View'. Instead of facing the central field as most of the others did, it stood apart at the furthest corner of the estate at the end of a short drive fringed by pine trees that have long since been cut down. These trees became so many eyries for me, the ladder-like set of their branches a positive invitation to climb them. My knees would be sticky and scented by the clear resinous gum their trunks exuded and as I lay in bed I could hear their branches, heavy-laden with dark pine needles, soughing on windy nights with a sound like the sea. In winter those branches would bow to the ground beneath their burden of snow.

These trees made a somewhat gloomy approach to what was a not unattractive house. From the end of the drive one could see its front porch of green-painted wood framed in an arc of dark trees. But the house was set at such an angle to the drive that its plain sash windows looked out across a tennis lawn and over the little town in the valley below to the gentle slope of Radnor, a mosaic of fields and copses that rose behind the village of Clyro beyond the Wye. Unlike the 'Sea Views' of so many coastal resorts, at least the house was honestly named. Beyond the house, the drive led to a small coach-house and stable with a hayloft above which fronted a paddock intended to furnish the necessary winter fuel supply for the horse transport. This stable was a singularly ugly building of cream-painted corrugated iron with green doors and windows. But at a time when the motor-car was beginning to oust the horse-drawn carriage for private transport, it must have been one of the latest buildings of its kind. In our time the only appropriate occupant of the stable was Meg, a diminutive Shetland pony which my parents bought for me in a misguided moment. She proved to be a vicious little brute with the habits of biting her rider in the leg, or crushing his foot against any convenient wall or tree. This effectually put me off riding for good and all. I have ever since preferred wheels to hooves.

My father, who at one time had been a keen amateur racing cyclist, greatly favoured two wheels (or at the most three) to four and throughout the war years the coach-house at Radnor View housed the two motor-cycles he had brought with him from Chester: a 2¾ h.p. solo A.J.S. for personal transport, and a huge unwieldy Williamson combination for family use. This last was a somewhat rare breed. It was powered by a flat twin water-cooled Douglas engine and had radiators mounted beside the front forks as on a Scott. In my recollection it was not particularly reliable and as a family we never motored very far afield. I cannot think what had prompted my father to buy it, as he was a devotee of A.J.S. motorcycles, maintaining that they were the finest machines in the world.

The house had a red-tiled roof and walls of rough-dressed local old red sandstone with brick quoins. At the front, these walls were practically invisible under a dense tangle of white flowering clematis and ivy. If one looks at old photograph albums it is surprising how many houses were densely clothed in creepers at this time. It cannot have been good for the masonry, making it impossible to see when it needed repointing, while many unwelcome insect visitors found their way in through the windows. These included earwigs of which I had a positive horror, having been told by nurse that they were liable to crawl into my ears and drive me mad.

As one entered the front door, my mother's drawing-room lay to the right while on the left was my father's smoking-room. This had a high fender topped by a padded leather seat surrounding the fireplace. On walls and shelves were numerous memorials of his roving life: an Australian boomerang and nulla-nulla of aborigine origin and a long stock-whip to remind him of his days 'down under'; a silver trophy won when playing polo for the Behar Light Horse in India; a length of whalebone, and the broken head of a harpoon recalling his empty-handed return from the Yukon expedition; a pelican's head mounted on a wooden shield from heaven knows where. A mahogany glass-fronted gun case housed his revolvers (one fitted with a long saloon barrel), a ·22 Winchester repeating rifle and a magnificent pair of shot guns – 16-bore Holland and Holland Royals. My father was a deadly shot who spurned a 12-bore as though it had been a blunderbuss. Shooting with the smaller 16s he could hold his own with any man. Much later, after my father's death, I became a sufficiently good shot myself to be able to appreciate the superb quality and balance of these guns, but since I could not use them in the manner my father had, I regretfully decided to sell them at a time when I was particularly hard-up. I should have got a great deal more for them had they been 12-bores.

Sometimes, to entertain his small son and to prove to himself that he still had the knack, my father would take his stock-whip down from its hook and out on to the tennis lawn. There, while I watched him goggle-eyed from a safe distance, he would whirl the long whip faster and faster about his head until it made a loud whistling noise. Then, with a quick flick of the wrist, the spinning circle would suddenly become a straight line and the lash would crack with a noise like a gun shot.

At the back of the house facing south were the dining-room, the kitchen and the servants' quarters where dwelt a housemaid and my beloved Welsh nurse, Mary Gwynne. The dining-room had a pair of French windows opening on to a small lawn, sunny and sheltered, where we frequently sat out in basket chairs in summer. A grass path flanked by herbaceous borders led away from this lawn and from it one could look across green fields to the foothills of the Black Mountains: wooded Mouse Castle to the left, Cusop Hill, with a solitary white cottage halfway down its steep slope, directly opposite and, away to the right beyond the deep cleft of Cusop Dingle, the hill oddly named the Haynault which had a curious crest of outcropping rocks. Of these three hills, only the first was a true outlier; the other two were merely the steep faces of a high, wide moorland which we called the plateau, a great windy, unenclosed and curlew-haunted sheepwalk of close, springy turf and bracken which served as a plinth for those two northern gables of the Black Mountain ridges, Pen y Beacon (or Hay Bluff) and Rhiw Wen.

Although the Black Mountains are in reality of no great height, nowhere substantially exceeding 2,000 ft, they appear to be far higher and wilder. There are two reasons for this. First, their most prominent escarpments face north and east and are therefore nearly always in shadow. Hence they appear to loom over the rich red fields, the pastures and orchards of Herefordshire as darkly menacing as a thunder cloud. Secondly, they have a perfection of outline and symmetry that is incomparably grand. So majestic are the curves by which their projecting bluffs stoop towards the plain below that one is reminded of a succession of great waves, petrified upon the instant of breaking.

Seen from beyond the Wye, from Clyro or from the Radnor Hills beyond, these mountains with their outer rampart of foothills compose what I always consider to be one of the finest landscapes in all Britain. It was a scene that continually drew Kilvert's eye while he was at Clyro. He gives one particularly fine description of a stormy late afternoon in March 1870 when, as he watched, the clouds that had veiled the mountains from sight all day suddenly lifted and dissolved to reveal the whole range glistening with snow in the light of a setting sun. 'One's first involuntary thought in the presence of these magnificent sights,' he wrote, 'is to lift up the heart to God and humbly thank Him for having made the earth so beautiful . . . I could have cried with the excitement of the overwhelming spectacle . . . it seemed to me as if one might never see such a sight again.'

From our much closer vantage at Cusop we were denied such splendours. With the exception of one portion of the high shoulder of Pen y Beacon which appeared in the cleft of Cusop Dingle, the mountains lay hidden behind their foothills. But at least it was that much easier to explore their high solitudes and somehow I was always conscious of their presence.

Gradually, I came to know this country intimately. My first walks were necessarily confined to the more immediate neighbourhood, but as I slowly gained stature and strength I was able to range further afield. From what my father subsequently told me, my birth had been a traumatic experience for my mother. Consequently, it was some time after I was born before she could be persuaded even to look at me. In the meantime, I would have died but for my father's affection and the care of my nurses. Hence it was upon the latter, and in particular my Welsh nurse, Mary Gwynne, that my affections were at first centred. It was she who accompanied me on my first walks at Cusop. Initially these were part walk, part pram ride and they almost invariably took us along the narrow road that closely followed the Dulas Brook up Cusop Dingle. Perhaps I should explain that 'dingle' means a deep and narrow valley, the equivalent of the Welsh 'cwm'. Like other local terms such as 'glat', meaning a stile or any other form of climbable gap in a hedge, 'dingle' became a part of my growing vocabulary. No matter how many times I went that way, I never grew tired of Cusop Dingle, for the flowers in the cottage gardens beside the road and the changing foliage of the many and varied trees that overhung the brook ensured that on no two occasions did it look the same. But above all I loved the Dulas Brook. It fell down its narrow valley in a succession of small waterfalls, shadowed pools and boulder-strewn stickles. It was spanned by many narrow wooden footbridges by which the people from the cottages and farms on the opposite bank gained access to the road. I loved to stand on these bridges, gazing down into dark pools, flecked with moving patterns of gold by the sunlight that filtered through the hazels overhead, looking for trout. I would spot them sinuously breasting the clear water with the lazy motion of trailing water weeds, swayed by the current. There were birds, too, to look for; wagtails and white-throated dippers bobbing on the boulders in mid-stream, shy ring-ouzels, and occasionally the azure flash of a kingfisher flying fast and low over the water.

At such times the brook seemed half asleep, its voice sunk to a murmur as soothing as the hum of bees. But after a heavy storm on the mountains where it had its source the Dulas would become suddenly and violently awake and this I found terribly exciting. A great torrent of tawny water would come rushing down, filling the whole valley with its thunder. Tree branches were varnished by the spray that rose from the larger falls like drifting steam and, on the surface of the pools, gobbets of foam spun giddily in the eddies. When such sudden spates subsided as quickly as they had come there were always changes to look for; here a tree had been undermined and had fallen across the stream, there a miniature landslide of red earth had altered the shape of a familiar pool.

When I was recovering from my recurrent bouts of bronchitis in the spring, Mary used to push me up the Dingle in an old Bath chair which I steered by the long handle that controlled the single pivoting front wheel. On such occasions I would persuade Mary to let me coast down on the return journey. Goodnaturedly, though somewhat rashly, she would consent to this practice, allowing me to disappear rapidly out of her sight. Although the gradient was nowhere steep, it was almost continuous, the road rough and the elderly vehicle quite unsuited to such speeds, having a high centre of gravity and no form of brake. Why it did not overturn I do not know, but, as there was no risk of meeting wheeled traffic, I was able to pick the best line through the corners. When I had eventually rolled to rest I would wait for the faithful Mary to appear, somewhat flushed and breathless, brushing her brown hair out of her eyes.

That the Dingle road was rough is not strictly a true statement. One stretch of about 150 yards on the lower and more frequented portion had been given a tarred surface by the wealthy owners of a neighbouring house, partly to silence the iron-tyred wheels of passing carts and partly to prevent white road dust from blowing over their garden. It was then the only road of its kind for many miles around and although it was apt to become disconcertingly soft and sticky in hot weather, I used to regard with wonderment its smooth and dustless surface.

Later, when my mother realised that I was approaching the age of rationality and was fully in control of my bodily functions, she began to take the place of Mary as my companion on these walks. Sometimes my father would accompany us, but usually he was too preoccupied in shooting or fishing. In this way we established a normal relationship and she began to usurp my father's place in my affections. In retrospect, this seems a little unfair, but it was simply a reversal of the normal shift in the proportion of affection a boy feels for his parents as he grows up.

These walks with my mother took us further and further afield; to the tree-crowned mound and vallum of Mouse Castle, to the top of Cusop Hill and finally to 'the plateau' and the Black Mountains beyond. In order to reach the latter we had to walk up Cusop Dingle to the point where the metalled road ended, turn right-handed, cross the Dulas by a footbridge, and then climb steeply by a rough track, now a completely overgrown watercourse, to a farm called New Forest. It was by this farm that we gained a track that led up to the high plateau past the little lonely shepherd's holding that we knew as Cock-a-Lofty. Although it entailed a considerable climb, it cannot have been much more than three miles from our house to the plateau and we often went up in late summer to pick whinberries or the rarer cranberries. But the occasion I remember most vividly must have been in early spring. All was fresh green below, but when we had climbed to Cock-a-Lofty it was to be rewarded with a sight such as had ravished Kilvert so many years before. For under a sky of cloudless blue all the wide plateau and the slopes beyond were white with new-fallen snow and lay glittering in the sunshine, the folds on the flanks of the mountains shadowed to an unbelievable shade of deepest blue. I remember sliding over the black surface of a small, frozen tarn.

The track that we struck at New Forest Farm on these occasions led down to Hay in one direction and in the other it climbed ever higher up the side of Pen y Beacon until it finally curved out of sight between the two peaks to cross the high saddle between them by the Gospel Pass. This is known in Welsh as Bwlch yr Efengel, the Pass of the Evangelists, because, it is said, the Apostles Peter and Paul once crossed it on their mission to bring the gospel of Christ to the Silures. The summit of this pass was too far for my small legs and I used often to wonder what undiscovered country lay beyond those gables of the mountains until, on one memorable summer's day, I saw it for the first time.

My mother's mother, 'Grannie Timperley', was staying with us and, as a special treat, my father had hired an open two-horse wagonette to take us over the pass. A large wicker picnic hamper was stowed on board and we all set off on a perfect morning in June. When we reached the plateau, the clink of hooves and the grinding of the steel-shod wheels fell silent on the smooth close-bitten turf of the track so that one could hear the creaking of the harness as the two horses toiled steadily upward along the flank of Pen y Beacon. As we climbed ever higher, a breathtaking view unfolded over the valley of the middle Wye to Radnor Forest and the mountains of Wales beyond. But when we eventually turned left-

handed and passed quickly through the narrow defile of
the Gospel Pass, we turned our backs upon this familiar
country and I found myself translated into a landscape
much smaller in scale but in my eyes far more fascinating
because it appeared so lonely, so secret and so strange.
This was my first glimpse of the Vale of Ewyas, that deep
and rich valley that the Black Mountains harbour in their
heart. The child is always captivated by the miniature,
and, after the broad prospect, suddenly to come upon
this small and exquisite landscape that the mountains
guarded so jealously was an experience I never forgot.

The head of the valley into which we had come was
wild and treeless, its steep slopes furrowed by a fan of
converging streams, but I could see below the first small
green fields with a glimpse of distant trees beyond and
as we slowly descended towards the valley floor we soon
left the open mountain for a narrow high-banked lane
where arching hazels made a tunnel of green shade. And
so we came to the lost hamlet of Capel-y-ffyn with its
tiny church and Baptist chapel. Here we turned aside to
visit the Monastery, scene of that ill-starred attempt by
Joseph Leycester Lyne, self-styled 'Father Ignatius', to
found a community of Anglican Benedictine monks.
Though tenantless, the Monastery buildings still
appeared externally to be in good order, for Father
Ignatius had died only some ten years before. The high
roof of the choir – the only portion of the great church
he planned that was actually built – still looked sound
and secure, though eventually its vaulting would fall,
covering the tomb of Ignatius, who lies buried beneath
the central aisle, under tons of masonry. Beside this

church, we saw the monastery bell, 'Big Bernard', still hanging within its wooden framework; how it was ever got up the narrow valley road is still a mystery to me. We saw, too, the white marble statue of Our Lady standing incongruous and ghostly in the corner of a field below the Monastery, marking the spot where she is alleged to have appeared to the brothers. This happening is commonly attributed to wishful thinking. Maybe so, but I will only say that if ever it is vouchsafed to man to see visions, then it would be in such a place as this valley whose very air seemed to a child to be numinous and charged with magic. That one of the remote mountain holdings nearby is called the Vision Farm is nothing to do with nineteenth-century mysticism but recalls some far older tradition.

I thought the Monastery, on the dark side of the valley and surrounded by gloomy pines, a sad, depressing place and was glad when we were rumbling on our way again along the narrow winding lane down the valley. The sun shone down out of a clear sky; there were wild strawberries and foxgloves growing in the hedge banks and through gateways in the hazels there were occasional glimpses of meadows carpeted with wild flowers; the creamy froth of meadowsweet; the purple spires of orchis. The further we went, the stronger sounded the voice of the stream below the lane, the taller and richer grew the trees until at length we turned aside and came to our destination – the ruined Priory of Llanthony, or 'The Abbey' as it is called in the valley. Here the picnic basket was unpacked and we lunched on the green turf beside the columns of the ruined nave.

No building in Britain has so majestical a setting as Llanthony. The valley hereabouts is at its widest and most luxuriant. Like some gigantic outflung lion's paw, the high, bracken-furred wall of Hatterall Hill encloses its richness in a majestic protective arc terminating in a steep fall. Its slopes were thickly sewn with sheep and in that breathless summer stillness the sound of their distant bleating mingled with the singing of birds in the valley below. Everything seemed to conspire to charm my five senses. Nor was this first childish impression in any way delusive. For since this first ever-memorable visit I have returned to the Vale of Ewyas countless times at all stages of my life and have seen it in every kind of weather and seasonal mood. Yet its beauty has never failed to equal my expectation; in fact and in recollection it was to prove an unfailing source of spiritual solace to me from that day to this.

It was after this first visit to Llanthony that I began to take part in those communal, Kilvert-like walks and picnic parties to which I have already referred. Among those who joined us on these outings were our neighbours, Major Herbert Armstrong and his wife, who lived in a large and ugly house of yellow brick called Mayfield on the road down to Hay. He was a solicitor though he usually wore his uniform and had what was called a 'military bearing'. He had singularly piercing blue eyes and used to read the lessons in Cusop church. I stood rather in awe of him. Little did we realise then that in the dapper Major we were harbouring a dangerous viper with poisoned fangs in our peaceful country nest.

A much more likeable companion on these picnics was Thomas Southwick, a retired inspector of schools, a mild, scholarly and kindly man with a grey beard and pince-nez. My father took to him although the two men were quite dissimilar in character. He used to stroll down the road on summer evenings for a quiet game of bowls with my father on our tennis lawn. I used to listen to the click of the woods and the soothing murmur of male voices as I lay in bed. Thomas Southwick became my tutor and each morning I trotted up the road through the Forty Acres to take my lessons in his study. He was an inspired teacher who taught me more than I ever learned subsequently at school.

I remember sitting at my mid-morning lesson in Mr Southwick's study when the steam hooter at the sawmills near Hay Station suddenly and unexpectedly blared. Why was it sounding so loud and so long at such a time? Thomas Southwick leaned back in his chair and sighed: 'Well, it's over at last,' he said. The date was 11th November 1918 and the Armistice had just been declared.

Later, when I came to realise fully the terrible carnage and agony of the Great War and that these years had been a time of the breaking of nations, it used to make me feel guilty to think how little the even tenor of our lives had been affected by it. I remember only my father, who was too old to serve, shaking his head over the headlines in the newspaper and the dark green blinds which we put up as a precaution against air raids, although no Zeppelin ever came within a hundred miles of Hay. Thanks to my father's proficiency with rod and gun, plus the produce of a large vegetable garden, we hardly felt the effects of food rationing. Our larder was always kept well supplied with fish and game in season. I recall sitting on the bank of the Wye and watching my father, within two hours, take three salmon, none of them under 15 lb, from the Wyecliff pool just above Hay. But, although he was an expert salmon fisherman, he much preferred trout fishing as calling for the greater skill and when my uncle Neville came to stay they would go off on trout fishing expeditions, fishing the Kentchurch Court water on the Monnow or, latterly, the Usk at Brecon. It was a disappointment to my father that I never took up fishing; I think I reacted against his total commitment to the sport.

Although there were – and still are – grouse on the Black Mountains, the population was never very great and as the 'Twelfth' came round my father's 'Royals' would be carefully dismantled and packed in their fitted travelling case ready for his annual pilgrimage to Scotland. There he would join a wealthy shooting friend named Holmes who each year rented Methven Castle in Perthshire. Highly coloured postcards of purple moors briefly reporting the 'bag' would arrive together with several brace of grouse to festoon our larder. Lack of refrigeration never worried my father who liked his game high. He used to maintain that grouse should hang until maggots appeared on the flags below. At other seasons my father found plenty of rough shooting locally. In Norfolk jacket, breeches, puttees and shooting boots, with a capacious shooting bag on his back and a cartridge belt round his waist, he would set off for a day's shooting, gun under arm and cocker spaniel trotting at heel. His cockers 'Don' and 'Flora' successively inhabited a kennel behind the stable and were not permitted to cross the threshold of the house. He never returned from these expeditions without at least a brace of pheasants or partridges, depending on the season.

We salted down farm butter in a great earthenware crock and my father bought two small piglets to fatten for the table. This, his only venture in livestock keeping, was only partially successful. For one of the pigs somehow contrived to fall into our compost pit where it proceeded to gorge itself on decaying lawn mowings until it practically burst and the local vet had to be called to put it out of its misery. Such misfortunes my father would dismiss with a sigh and a shrug as an example of what he termed the 'Rolt luck'. In fact this luck, or rather ill-luck, was really due to the fact that the Rolt ability to excel in any form of field sport was matched by an almost total incapacity to deal efficiently with anything which had to do with the practical business of living.

The seasons also brought the fruits of the field: wild strawberries in profusion on the high hedge banks at midsummer; mushrooms in quantity from the old pastures; whinberries from the mountains and, of course, blackberries. Gathering hazel-nuts was a favourite pastime of mine on autumn walks in the deep lanes. When I brought the nuts home I used to pack them into tins and then bury them in the earth of the garden, like a squirrel, digging them up at Christmas. I used to think they tasted better that way.

From the boundary hedge of our small paddock, one looked across a couple of meadows to a farm beneath the slopes of Mouse Castle. This farm, which I used to call 'Lididiway' (it was really Lidiart-y-Wain), was unusually large for this district of small farms. It was of very ancient origin. There were traces of a moat and ranges of barns, bartons and stables all of local old red sandstone with walls of massive thickness. Local people used to say that they had originally been built to keep out the wolves. Whether this was true or no, it was like a farm in a story book, a mixed farm of the traditional kind with arable fields under oats, wheat and roots and with green pastures heavily stocked with red Hereford bullocks, milking cows and, of course, the ubiquitous sheep. At the farm there were pigs in the styes and a great stable full of horses, for everything was done by horse-power. Ducks and geese swam in the large pond which was part of the old moat, while the farmyard was full of scratching chickens, turkeys strutting among them with an air of affronted dignity.

I became friendly with the son of this farmer (I cannot now recall his name), a boy of about my own age, and used often to slip away across the fields to join him. Wet or fine, that farm with its great barns was a wonderful place for boys. On one occasion we succeeded in mounting and riding a couple of rams. I returned home reeking with the smell of their oily fleeces to the consternation of my mother and Mary. In the cart shed was every kind of horse-drawn vehicle from light gigs and traps to great four-wheeled Herefordshire harvest wagons whose massive wheels were not tyred but shod with a double row of iron strakes. There was also a type of two-wheeled harvest cart which we called a gambo.*

We used to help at haysel and harvest, pitching until the load grew too high for our small arms, or setting the corn sheaves in stook. And we loved to ride back to the farm, sprawled on top of the loaded wains, their loads brushing the hazels as they lumbered down the narrow lanes. I remember – it must have been at the height of the U-boat blockade in 1917, I think – that I first saw a Fordson tractor at plough on this farm. I little thought then that this was the thin end of a very large wedge that would drive the horse from the farm altogether within my lifetime, leaving gaily painted wagons and harness bright with polished ornament to rot and to tarnish.

Apart from my friend the farmer's boy, I knew few local children for I was, and still am, an unsociable animal and I always disliked children's parties. Occasions of this sort were reserved for Christmas when we invariably went to Chester to stay with my aunt Augusta and her doctor husband. Our neighbours may have thought me a lonely child, but solitary would have been a better word for I was never consciously lonely. Nor do I recall reading much as lonely children are apt to do. For although Thomas Southwick had given me an excellent grounding in the first two of the three Rs, I never felt

---

* The true gambo, however, originated in Radnorshire where it was designed for use in steeply sloping fields. This Radnorshire gambo was part cart part sledge with a pair of massive forewheels and a pair of large bosses behind to act as runners. It would be drawn uphill on its wheels and come down on its runners with the wheels locked.

the need to escape into imaginary worlds conjured up by other minds. Of my first four years in Chester I retained only a few shadowy memories like a random collection of faded snapshots. It was this little world of the Welsh Border that I discovered for myself and made peculiarly my own. When, years later, I first read that famous meditation of Thomas Traherne which begins: 'The corn was orient and immortal wheat, which never should be reaped, nor was ever sown', I knew it to be a superbly articulate expression of all that I had felt as a child. It is said that the child is father to the man; certainly this 'first Light which shined in my infancy' affected me profoundly for the rest of my life. It was something which I learned to set my course by.

But I could not live in paradise forever, or, as my nurse would say tritely when I was reluctant to come to bed on a summer evening, 'All good things have got to come to an end, Master Tom.' I had to go to school; I had to learn, as Traherne puts it, 'the dirty devices of this world'.

Canal Crusade

Before the war, when I first had the optimistic idea of trying to earn my living as a writer, I had thought of this new career simply as a source of creative satisfaction and as a means of achieving that complete independence and privacy which I had always craved. Strange though it may seem, it had never occurred to me that there was an inescapable corollary to this neat scheme which was the price of its success. Books need readers; I could not make a living by writing the kind of books I wanted to write without publicizing the things I loved and, incidentally, without publicizing myself. In the modern world, even the least dazzling beam of public limelight can prove as lethal as gamma rays, corroding the personality of the 'private man' with the most subtle of poisons. And, like so many poisons, this one is addictive; men seek it as desperately as any drug. It is also isolating, cutting men off from normal, unselfconscious relationships with all except a few most intimate friends. As for writing about well-loved things or places, in our overcrowded island this can be tantamount to giving them the kiss of death. It was the reception of *Narrow Boat* and the shoals of letters I received as a result that first made me realize that there were such unforeseen strings attached to my projected way of earning a living, although it would be hypocritical to say that I was not gratified. Yet I still had no inkling of – and, indeed, had never considered – the possible long-term effect of the book upon its subject, the English canals.

I had known the canals for fifteen years and lived on them for five, and in that time I had come to love them and their people. For me they represented the equivalent of some uncharted, arcadian island inhabited by simple, friendly and unselfconscious natives where I could free myself from all that I found so uncongenial in the modern world. It seems fantastic to me now that when I was writing *Narrow Boat* I did not realize that I was putting this island firmly on the chart. The book was described by one reviewer as 'an elegy of classic restraint'. If it was elegiac it was because I realized that this old and simple world of the canals was too fragile to resist for very long the relentless march of technology captained by modern economic theory. But I certainly never foresaw how very soon the natural life of that world would come to an end. Admittedly, on some canals such as the Worcester & Birmingham, commercial traffic was visibly failing; but on many other narrow canals of the Midlands traffic had increased substantially, so that I saw no reason to suppose that it would so rapidly decline into extinction in the post-war world.

Among the many letters I received following the publication of *Narrow Boat* was one suggesting the forma- tion of a voluntary society ('something like the friends of Canterbury cathedral') to campaign for the greater use of canals and proposing a meeting to discuss the idea further. This letter came from an address in Bloomsbury and was signed Robert Fordyce Aickman. Such a notion had never occurred to me, but anything which might help the canal boaters could not, I thought, fail to be a good thing so I welcomed the idea enthusiastically. Had I not acted so impulsively I might have questioned whether it was such a good idea and so have avoided the storms which lay ahead. But at this time my experience of running voluntary organizations was extremely limited. It was exclusively confined to the Committee of the Vintage Sports Car Club before the war where there had been no clashes of temperament. On the contrary, the atmosphere there had been so harmonious that all the issues discussed were settled by mutual agreement and never had to be put to the vote. I assumed in my innocence that such a happy state of affairs was the rule rather than the exception, but I was to learn otherwise. The launching of the Inland Waterways Association, as we named it, and its promotion, was to become my major preoccupation for the first five years after the war. But although they were years of considerable achievement, some of them memorable, they led finally to a sense of growing frustration and ended in complete exasperation. Now that time has distanced these events I can see that they had their funny side, so that what appeared then to be a tragedy appears in retrospect a black comedy. There is certainly a ludicrous element about our foibles and frailties however infuriating they may be at the time; nevertheless, there can be no doubt that our infant Association would have had a much more healthy childhood had there not been so much bickering among its parents.

At a preliminary meeting in London at which Robert Aickman assumed the chair, my old friend Charles

Hadfield and I were elected Vice-Chairman and Honorary Secretary respectively. Charles Hadfield has since become famous as a canal historian. He, also, had written to me as a result of *Narrow Boat* and I was responsible for drawing him in. After this first meeting I returned to *Cressy* filled with enthusiasm and bashed out on my typewriter a Constitution and Rules for the new Association, a booklet, to be illustrated with Angela's photographs, entitled *The Future of the Waterways*, which set forth our aims, and a leaflet-cum-entry-form for distribution to likely members. These three efforts were approved at our next meeting, although the first two were subsequently destined to be much revised by another hand. Each of us compiled a list of names and addresses of possible members to whom the leaflet would be sent. Mine included all my *Narrow Boat* correspondents, for I had fortunately kept all their letters which made a formidable pile.

Because Angela and I had arranged our Irish canal trip before the new Association was first mooted, I was not in England but afloat on the Shannon when the new canal crusade was launched by the sending out of the leaflets in the late spring of 1946. I was told that subscriptions were coming in well; but coupled with this came the news that Charles Hadfield had resigned as Vice-Chairman. This was disturbing and saddening because I had taken an immediate liking to Charles who has been a very good friend of mine from that day to this. Remote from the centre of events, I could not then fathom the reason for his withdrawal, though I realized later that this was only the first ominous cloud in a sky presaging future storms. Charles had acutely sized up a situation that was still not clear to me.

We returned to England and Banbury in September to find that *Cressy* had still not been dry-docked but was lying at her moorings exactly as we had left her three months before. This was tiresome because it was not possible for us to live aboard while she was on the dock. We were forced to hire a caravan which we parked in the boatyard while the work was done, finding it very cramped and inconvenient after our boat. As autumn drew on we also realized that it was very much colder. We appreciated then as never before how effective an insulator water is, for although we turned on heat in that caravan until our heads were bursting, our legs remained obstinately numb from the knees down due to the cold that struck up through the floor. We were back on *Cressy* again by mid-November fortunately, because that winter of 1946–7 turned out to be the longest, coldest and hardest we had ever known. For weeks *Cressy* was locked in ice several inches thick, usually covered with a deep layer of snow, and it was early March before the weather broke with tremendous gales and floods. However, our boat was extremely warm and snug, and in this respect we were a great deal better off than most landsmen during that dismal winter of prolonged power cuts and fuel shortages. But it was a hard time for our friends the boaters, many of whom were frozen in beside us. Most of them found temporary employment with Banbury Corporation, clearing the snow from the streets. Even so, the 'Number Ones' – those who owned their own boats – were forced to draw upon their precious 'docking money', a sum set aside for the repair of their boats. Yet they managed to remain remarkably cheerful and many a pleasant evening we spent with them in the bars of 'The Leather Bottle' or 'The Struggler'; men and women – never together but always separately – dancing to the music of a melodeon that was passed from hand to hand among the boatmen.

'The Struggler' was a small and outwardly insignificant street-corner pub in a back-street which was much frequented by the boaters and also, at fair times, by gypsies and horse-dealers. It had the unusual sign of a globe with a man's legs protruding from one side of it and his head the other. It bore the legend: 'Oh Lord help me through this World'. This used to strike me as singularly appropriate for its roving, impoverished but undaunted customers, none of whom fitted into the neat, organized pattern of modern society. I once described a typical evening spent in 'The Struggler' so I will not do so again. I did not then name either the pub or the place for obvious reasons. But now there is no further need for such reticence. Developers have destroyed 'The Struggler' and even if they had not, its bar would never again see such a company because the boaters and their boats are all gone. Most of the gypsies and horse-dealers have gone into limbo with them. In the tidy, aseptic world that we have made there is no place for them.

It was not only with the canal boaters and gypsies that I became acquainted during successive winters spent at moorings at Tooley's Yard. I never forgot my first love, railways, and got to know a G.W.R. relief signalman named Billy Bevington. A relief signalman must be

prepared, often at short notice, to stand in for any signalman who may happen to be ill or on leave. This meant
that Billy had an intimate knowledge of every box on
the Paddington–Birmingham main line within cycling
distance of Banbury. I used to receive cryptic messages
from him such as 'Banbury Junction this week 2 till 10',
which meant that he would be pleased to welcome me
to that box at any time between those hours. Sometimes
on such visits he would sit down in the home-made chair
(essential in any signal box) by the stove and leave me
to work the block instruments, set the road and 'pull the
sticks off'. In this way I gained experience which would
eventually become virtually unrepeatable, at any rate
on a main line such as this, owing to the installation of
modern electrical signalling systems. What impressed
me was the strength of tradition on the railways, and
also the comparative crudity of the old manual system
on which railway safety depended. To illustrate the first
point, Billy habitually referred to a stopping train that
ran 'all stations' between Birmingham and Oxford as
'the Parly', a name going back to the early days of
railways when a Parliamentary Act compelled reluctant
companies such as the G.W.R. to cater for third-class
passengers. As to crudity I vividly remember one Saturday afternoon at Banbury North Box when the signal
wire of the down starter parted with a melodious twang
as he was 'pulling his sticks off' for a 'runner' (a
Paddington–Birmingham non-stop express). Knowing
there was no hope of getting a linesman out at such
short notice on a Saturday, Billy handed me an old pair
of pliers and a coal hammer saying, 'Go down below

and see what you can do about it, Tom.' Obediently I passed through the little door beneath the box stairway and threaded my way through a maze of point rods, signal wires, bell cranks and interlocking bars until I had found the broken wire. I never realized until then how extremely tough signal wire is, especially when one has to attack it with totally inadequate tools; the knowledge that time was not on my side did not help matters either. 'Look sharp' called a voice from above as I sweated and struggled. At last I managed to form the two broken ends into rough hooks which, by slacking off the wire adjuster, I managed to link together. 'Try it now,' I called up, 'but for God's sake take it easy.' Fortunately it was only a short pull and to my relief my extempore repair held, the lever swung over into the 'off' position and I emerged from the box to see for myself that the signal arm had obediently dropped. Hardly had I done so than the train, drawn by an immaculate 'Castle' class locomotive, flashed past me with a roar, a brief glimpse of thrashing coupling rods, the echo of a whistle just closed and the swift rhythm of bogie wheels over rail joints. I caught a momentary glimpse of passengers taking tea in the restaurant car and thought wryly that but for my pliers and coal hammer their train would have come to a grinding halt.

At Banbury Junction Box there existed a very curious device in the shape of a hand-cranked dynamo, the purpose of which was to provide power assistance for a set of points a very long way away from the box. The junction concerned was that between the G.W.R. main line and the Great Central Branch from Woodford and the point in question admitted freight trains from off this branch into Banbury hump marshalling yard. Whenever the lever controlling it needed pulling off, Billy would call, 'Wind away, Tom, go on – faster!' The whole operation reminded me of one of those children's toys that derives its motion from the energy stored in a heavy flywheel. The principle was exactly the same. But by far the most interesting and unusual signal box in the Banbury area stood close beside the Oxford canal just outside Fenny Compton station. It was islanded between the G.W.R. main line on the one hand and the single line of the S.M.J.,* now part of the L.M.S. system, on the other. It was a 'facing both ways' box with G.W.R. type block instruments and frame on one side and on the other a small L.M.S. frame with its accompanying tablet instruments to control the single line sections.

That bitter first winter at Banbury I was a member of a deputation, led by the late lamented A. P. Herbert (who had agreed to be the Association's President), which had been formed for the purpose of visiting the then Minister of Transport to urge upon him the greater use of canals in the post-war world. I recall this because our appointment was in the morning which meant our catching an early train from Banbury to Paddington. Woken by our alarum clock at a godless hour, we dressed by lamplight in unfamiliar and uncomfortable London clothes and then looked out to see, in the first pale light of dawn, that there had been a fresh and heavy fall of

* S.M.J. stood officially for Stratford-upon-Avon & Midland Junction but unofficially for Slow, Mouldy & Jolting. The railway along with the box as I knew it has long ago disappeared.

snow in the night which had covered the boat, the frozen canal and the stacks of seasoning oak planks in the boat-yard in a blanket of white eight inches deep. We floundered across the yard to the high wooden gate giving on to Factory Street to find it still padlocked. Instead of climbing it, how much easier, we thought, to walk across the frozen canal to the towpath. I led the way boldly and immediately my left leg went straight through the snow and ice into the canal up to the knee. As luck would have it I had picked the one place in the canal where the ice had been broken the evening before for the purpose of watering a horse. If we were to catch our train there was nothing for it but to press on, so we hurried through the snow to the station, my sodden trouser leg flapping against my shin and canal water squelching inside my shoe. Our hope of finding an empty compartment on the train was vain, and our travelling companions were somewhat disconcerted when I removed my shoe and sock and placed them against the radiator under the seat. But for their presence I would have removed my trousers as well. Fortunately there was just time to give them a hurried ironing and pressing before the deputation left for Berkeley Square House. It was all in a good cause, or so we hoped.

When a belated spring eventually arrived, we decided that the time had come to do some campaigning for the new Association by deed instead of merely by word. This was just before the canals were nationalized, and we decided that two of the railway-owned canals, the Stratford and the Welsh Section of the Shropshire Union, should be the targets for our attack. We had learned that the Lifford drawbridge at the northern end of the Stratford Canal, which we had passed under with difficulty on our way to Tardebigge in 1941, had since collapsed under heavy road traffic and that the G.W.R. had replaced it by a 'temporary' fixed steel structure which made the canal impassable by anything larger than a canoe. Unlike the southern end of this canal between its junction with the Grand Union at Kingswood and Stratford-upon-Avon which was then in an advanced state of decay, this northern section had been used in comparatively recent times by commercial traffic trading between London and the south of Birmingham. The trade in cocoa beans and chocolate 'crumb' from London docks to the Cadbury factory at Bournville had been a notable example of such movements, and I then saw no reason why such trade might not be resumed provided the canal could be opened up.

In challenging the might of the G.W.R. we had one trump card to play which has now, most unfortunately, been lost – a statutory right of navigation.* We therefore

* This right was written into most, though not all, of the original canal Acts. The Act for the Derby Canal was one of the exceptions. This enabled the Derby Canal Company to defeat a plot, laid between Brigadier H. E. Hopthrow of I.C.I., Mr Mallender, Managing Director of the Derby Gas, Light & Coke Company and myself to bring a pair of boats laden with coal on to the eastern section of the canal. Somehow the canal company got wind of this scheme and foiled us by the simple expedient of chaining and padlocking the gates of the entrance lock at the junction with the Erewash Canal at Sandiacre. Shortly afterwards the Company applied for and obtained an abandonment order on the grounds that there had been no commercial traffic on their waterway for many years.

persuaded Lord Methuen, who was a member of the new Association, to put down a question about Lifford bridge in the House of Lords. It is ironical that after nationalization such a question would have been brushed aside in the House as 'a matter for the day-to-day concern of the transport authority'. In 1947, however, it was quite a different story and it obviously caused quite a stir at Paddington. For the reply was that Lifford bridge would be lifted at any time on notice of an intended passage being given. So we duly gave notice of our intention to pass through the canal on 20 May.

Of this and subsequent voyages I have an accurate record because I continued to keep as complete a log of each day's journeying as I had done on our honeymoon voyage in 1939. I see from this that we slipped our moorings at Banbury on 14 May and moored in the basin at Kingswood on Saturday the 17th. We were surprised to see an empty motor narrow boat, *Bilster*, also moored in this deserted basin and discovered that the G.W.R. had chartered this craft from the Grand Union Canal Company's Hatton Maintenance Depot with the object of putting her through ahead of us to clear a passage and so avert the adverse publicity which might result if *Cressy* got hopelessly stuck or was damaged. The G.W.R. was obviously taking the affair seriously. Already the venture was attracting some attention and the next day's entry in my log reads briefly: 'Sunday, 18th May. Poured practically all day. Lay at Kingswood troubled by reporters and I.W.A. members.' This led me to reflect wryly on the contrast with our previous voyage in 1941 when we had slipped through the canal unnoticed and without any fuss. But I consoled myself with the thought that it was all in a good cause.

The next day dawned fine but cold and overcast. At 10 o'clock the *Bilster* set off up the Lapworth locks with G.W.R. and G.U.C. engineers on board. Knowing that even an empty boat of this type draws more at the stern end than did *Cressy*, from my previous experience of the canal I did not fancy her chances of getting through and my fear was that she might become hopelessly stuck in a bridge-hole and so block the canal for us. I decided to give her a good start, so we did not leave until 2 p.m. The state of the canal had certainly deteriorated since 1941, for although we climbed the nineteen locks without incident, the weed in the long summit pound was so thick that for about a mile in the neighbourhood of Hockley Heath we had to resort to bow-hauling from the overgrown towpath. Then conditions improved somewhat so that we were able to go forward slowly under our own power once more until we tied up for the night beside the junction of the canal feeder channel from Earlswood Lakes.

We had not travelled very far next morning before I saw ahead of us the sight I had most feared – the *Bilster* firmly wedged in a bridge-hole. A number of men were either pulling or shoving without result, and though we added our weight to theirs, still she would not budge, being obviously hard aground on a mound of debris. From the other side of the high towpath hedge came the unmistakable sound of a Fordson tractor at plough, and we succeeded in persuading its driver to unhitch it and drive it on to the towpath. Quite how this difficult manoeuvre was achieved I cannot now remember. For, as anyone familiar with canals will know, there are no gateways between fields and canal towpaths as local farmers and landowners had no desire to provide free pasturage for boatmen's horses. However, I have a press photograph to prove that this feat was achieved, where-upon the Fordson successfully pulled *Bilster* through the bridge. We then followed suit, man-handling *Cressy* as I was not going to risk a broken propeller.

We had hardly got fairly under way once more before, on rounding a bend, we saw *Bilster* once again, not stuck in a bridge-hole this time but aground in the middle of the canal. The only thing to be done was to try and edge *Cressy* past, and no one was more surprised than I was when this manoeuvre succeeded. Moreover, when alongside I was able to pass a line over *Bilster*'s fore-end stud and make it fast, which successfully pulled her off. I now had this official 'trail-blazer' in tow, a somewhat humiliating situation for her charterers though it proved to be short-lived. As we approached the next bridge-hole I stopped my propeller as a precaution and sure enough we grounded at the stern. Although we managed to haul her over the obstruction without much difficulty it was obvious that the *Bilster* would be in worse trouble here than ever before. Her captain had obviously weighed up the situation and had come to the same conclusion, for he signalled me to cast off the tow and leave him to his fate. What the end of his story was we never knew, for that was the last we saw of the *Bilster*.

We went ahead very slowly and cautiously. There was always in my mind the fear that *Cressy* might hit some underwater obstruction, 'knock a bottom up' and sink ignominiously and expensively in the middle of the canal. The thought of those muddy waters slowly rising over the floor of our carpeted saloon and up the spines of the lowest bookshelf was a nightmare prospect on which I did not care to dwell. Indeed this whole venture was rather like taking a long-cherished old family motor car on some tough, chassis-breaking reliability trial. But at last we reached King's Norton tunnel without untoward incident, and soon after we had emerged from its darkness the infamous Lifford 'drawbridge' appeared ahead. Unlike the previous occasion when we had passed this way, it presented an animated scene. The steel decking which had replaced the old wooden bridge had been jacked up on to wooden packing by a posse of overalled G.W.R. gangers who were standing by, and the towpath was lined with spectators, mostly press reporters and photographers. The gang had evidently decided to do no more work on their jacks than was absolutely necessary, for there were only a couple of inches to spare over our roof tank as *Cressy* was slowly manhandled beneath the girders. I remembered the shoal beyond the bridge on which *Cressy* had grounded heavily on the previous occasion. It consisted of ashes ejected from the boiler house of a factory beside the towpath, and we soon found that it had grown in the five years that had since elapsed. But at least there was no lack of manpower this time. Normally, I dislike spectators when engaged upon exploits of this kind, but there are occasions when they can be useful and this was one of them. If the last hundred yards of canal to the junction stop lock had been completely dry, I think sheer enthusiasm would have dragged us there. Nevertheless, after the crowds and the questioning, it was a relief to plunge like a rabbit into a burrow into the dark depths of West Hill tunnel and so escape from it all. We were on our own again.

This episode was only the opening chapter in the saga of Lifford bridge, for had we allowed matters to rest there is no doubt at all that the status quo would have remained undisturbed. Somehow, we had to ensure a series of repeat performances until it dawned on the canal owners (soon to be the British Transport Commission) that it might be cheaper to reconstruct the bridge than continually to send large gangs of men to jack it up. So we begged all members of our infant Association to take their boats through the Stratford Canal, but unfortunately the number of members with suitable boats was in those days very small. One of this minority who had a go was Peter Scott. He had a narrow boat converted by a boatyard in Birmingham with the object that, when moored on the Gloucester & Berkeley Ship Canal, she would form a convenient hostel for students visiting his then newly formed Wildfowl Trust at Slimbridge. This boat, the *Beatrice*, followed the design of *Cressy* very closely, even to the paintwork and the fitting of a Model 'T' Ford engine. The only difference was that this engine drove a small propeller directly instead of copying Kyrle Willans's arrangement of reduction drive to a large propeller. This proved to be mistaken, for putting *Beatrice* full astern had no effect whatever on her forward progress, the little propeller being about as much use as an egg whisk.

When *Beatrice* was ready to make her maiden voyage from Birmingham to Slimbridge, instead of going by the direct route, Peter dutifully took her down to Kingswood and thence through the Stratford Canal. On this occasion I joined *Beatrice* on the Lapworth Locks and my voyage as 'pilot' was made ever memorable, not by any untoward occurrence on the Stratford Canal but by an episode in West Hill tunnel. We had just about reached the middle of this long tunnel when I heard the engine die, the ensuing silence broken only by an echoing exclamation from Peter who was at the tiller. I hurried aft and soon discovered the cause of the trouble. He had grossly underestimated *Beatrice*'s thirst for fuel. Her fuel tank was completely dry, nor had anyone thought to lay on any spare cans. There was nothing for it but to man-handle the boat out of the tunnel.

The Worcester & Birmingham Canal was, I think, unique among the old canal companies in possessing its own telephone system throughout. Although this had long ago fallen into disuse, the metal brackets that had carried the insulators still existed along the crown of the tunnel roof. By standing on the cabin, pushing against each bracket in turn while I walked aft and then running for'ard to wait for the next bracket to come up, I found I could keep the boat moving at about half its normal speed. By the time we finally emerged from the south end of the tunnel, dusk was falling and I was not only exhausted but black as a sweep from the accumulation of soot that the vanished steam tug *Droitwich* had left on the tunnel roof. It was noticeable that the other I.W.A. members present on this occasion took no part in these proceedings but remained below drinking tea, content to leave it to Peter and myself to extricate them from this predicament. I have never 'legged' a boat through a canal tunnel in the traditional manner, but this experience was the next best thing and gave me a very fair idea of the sheer physical effort involved despite the fact that *Beatrice* was only the equivalent of a half-empty boat.

My 1947 assault on the Stratford Canal was only the first stage of a much more ambitious and venturesome voyage. Ever since I had experienced her first steam trials on the Welsh Canal in 1929, I had determined that one day I would pilot *Cressy* over Telford's great aqueduct across the Vale of Llangollen at Pont Cysyllte. Ten years later I had been foiled in the attempt by the outbreak of war, and now I was going to try again. In the meantime, however, the outcome of this venture had become very much more uncertain. No boats had voyaged from Hurleston Junction to Llangollen since before the war and, what was more, in 1944 the L.M. & S.R. had obtained Parliamentary powers which enabled the company to abandon the entire canal. Boats were permitted to enter it on sufferance, but the 1944 Act had extinguished the right of navigation. This meant that if *Cressy* sank, became hopelessly stuck or encountered an obstruction like Lifford bridge, I could obtain no legal redress, nor could I invoke any aid from the company. Once past Hurleston Junction, where the canal joins the main line of the Shropshire Union Canal, it would literally become a case of sink or swim.

After a short stay in brilliantly fine weather on our old moorings at Tardebigge, we locked down the famous 'thirty and twelve' en route for Worcester and the river Severn. At Diglis, Worcester, we swung right-handed on to the river and headed upstream in the direction of Stourport. At that time some friends of ours were living at Shrawley Wood House which lies close beside the west bank of the Severn just below Stourport. They joined us at Worcester, the idea being that, after luncheon on board, they would travel with us as far as Shrawley where we would moor up for the night so that they could entertain us to dinner. This had seemed an excellent idea, but it proved singularly difficult to carry out as anyone familiar with the high and thickly overgrown banks of the Severn will appreciate. The tremendous wash created by the many tanker barges that were then using the river added to the hazards of such an uncongenial mooring. Nevertheless we contrived to moor eventually beside the mouth of the Dick brook, and in this way I discovered the mysterious ruins of the mason's lock chambers built by Andrew Yarranton when he made the brook navigable in 1652. The course of the brook is so narrow and tortuous, the lock (or half-lock?) chambers so large and massive, that the whole set-up was a profound puzzle to me then as it still puzzles industrial archaeologists today.

Happily no harm came to *Cressy* at her somewhat risky mooring, and next morning we were soon locking up through the two large locks at Stourport which link the Severn with the terminal basin of the Staffordshire & Worcestershire Canal. We now intended to follow this as far as its junction with the 'main line' of the Shropshire Union at Autherley. This particular length of canal carried a very heavy traffic that was almost entirely horse drawn, for the power station at Stourport then took the bulk of its coal by water from the Cannock coalfield. This traffic was worked exclusively by what the long-distance canal boaters used to call, not without a certain disdain, 'Joey boatmen' – men who crewed the short-haul 'day-boats' peculiar to the canal system of the Black Country. More crudely built than the long-distance craft, the diminutive cabins of these day-boats were never used as homes but only as shelters for the crew of two during the day. The 'turn' from Gailey to Stourport was the longest to be worked by such craft and it was organized in two shifts, one gang working the boats between Gailey and the 'Stewponey Inn' where they handed over a loaded boat to their mates for the remainder of the journey, picking up an empty boat for the return journey.

We also saw on this canal a very significant relic of the canal past. This was the *Symbol*, an old Shropshire Union Canal Carrying Company horse-drawn fly-boat. She was now drably painted and bore the letters 'L.M. & S.R.' on her cabin sides, but her graceful lines and the fact that her name was carved on her stern made her origin unmistakable. Worked by two men, she was carrying general cargo and assorted parcels – the sort of traffic that once travelled 'fly' – between an L.M.S. Canal depot in the Black Country and Stourport. The *Symbol* was thus an inexplicable survivor of the long-defunct Shropshire Union Canal Carrying Company. With the coming of nationalization it quickly vanished; why such a traffic movement had survived for so long it is hard to say.

Competition between rival railway companies is probably the answer.

Although it was obvious that the *Symbol* was an anachronism, the traffic in coal to Stourport power station seemed such a logical movement that we had no doubts about its future. Evidently the newly appointed Docks & Inland Waterways Executive had no doubts either, for one of its first acts after nationalization was to dredge the whole canal between Gailey and Stourport. Hardly had this costly exercise been completed when the National Coal Board and the Central Electricity Generating Board agreed between them that future supplies of coal to Stourport should go by rail or road, and the coal drops beside the canal at Gailey were promptly demolished. This was a typical example of the follies that so soon followed upon nationalization, and it explains why our experience in 1947 was so soon to become a part of history. To see a wide and dusty towing path trampled by the hoof prints of many horses, to smell horse dung and to see the 'eloquent grooves' worn in metal rubbing strips by innumerable tow lines still bright from constant use, such trifles, once so commonplace in the canals, were never to be experienced again. Next year, when we passed that way, the traffic had vanished; weeds were already encroaching on the disused towpath, and the bright rope grooves had grown dull.

Our journey up the main line of the Shropshire Union from Autherley Junction was uneventful and we arrived at Nantwich to find that the entrance to the basin had been dredged out since our previous visit; so, to our relief, we were able to find a good mooring in the basin.

It was here we learnt that we were to have company on our voyage up the Welsh Canal: already moored in the basin was the small cabin cruiser *Heron* owned by the Grundy family of Liverpool. With the help of their two sons, Christopher and Martin, Mr and Mrs Grundy had decided to venture up the Welsh Canal and see how far they could get. As we had precisely the same intention we agreed there and then to set off together so that we could render each other assistance as necessary.

We had both heard a rumour that the wooden draw-bridge over the canal at Wrenbury had been damaged and could not be lifted. On the previous day, however, we had moored at Hack Green Locks on the main line whence it was but a short walk over to Wrenbury to inspect the bridge. We found, much to our surprise, that repairs had been completed the previous day, so we were able to reassure the Grundys that at least one obstacle had been removed.

Anticipating difficulty, I had equipped us with new spare cotton lines and a set of pulley blocks which were soon to prove their worth. At first everything went deceptively smoothly; we climbed successfully up the locks at Hurleston and Swanley and found the travelling between them much better than we had expected. It was at Lock No. 9, Baddiley, that the first serious hitch occurred when *Cressy* stuck fast half-way into the empty chamber.

It is a weakness of the orthodox design of a masonry lock chamber that its side walls are apt to be forced inwards owing to the action of frost in the surrounding ground. That the disused Welsh Canal locks had been affected in this way by two very severe winters in the past six years was a contingency that I had failed to take into account. A narrow boat slides into a narrow lock chamber with only inches to spare at the best of times, so it does not need much deformation to create an impasse such as now occurred. Despite the efforts of helpful lengthmen, using extra lines and the pulley blocks, or alternately lifting and dropping the top gate paddles to create a 'flush', *Cressy* refused to budge. Fortunately, however, the lower pound was a short one and the Baddiley lock keeper finally suggested lowering its level by drawing off water at the lock below. It was a risky expedient, for either *Cressy* might fail to drop with the water level or, if too much water was released, she could come to rest on the bottom sill. Happily neither of these disasters occurred and the device worked; *Cressy* suddenly dropped free and floated easily into the lock. But as the lock was filled, how anxiously we watched to ensure that she continued to rise with the water!

As our boat slowly rose above the upper gate, our hearts sank at the prospect before us. The canal ahead appeared to contain more weed than water, so much so that it looked solid enough to walk on. Even by frequent reversals to unwind the weed from the propeller, it was impossible to make progress at more than a snail's pace; while *Heron*, with her small propeller, was an even worse case. We ended up with *Heron* in tow behind *Cressy* while every available hand bow-hauled both from the towpath, our engine giving what assistance it could. Matters were made more difficult by the fact that the trouble at the lock had undoubtedly lowered the water level quite considerably. We therefore soon agreed to call it a day

in the hope that overnight the water would rise somewhat and so make the going a little easier.

At this point I should explain why, during the whole
of this first voyage up the Welsh Canal, we were dogged
by a persistent shortage of water. The canal draws its
water supply from the river Dee at the so-called 'Horse-
shoe Falls', actually a diversion weir built by Thomas
Telford, the engineer of the canal, at Llantisilio. The
original Ellesmere Canal Act which authorized construction contained a clause which stipulated that this water
was to be used for navigational purposes only, and
eventually returned to the river at Chester. In the 1940s,
however, the Dee Conservators discovered that the canal
owners, the L.M. & S. Railway, were selling canal water
in considerable volume to the Monsanto Chemical Company whose works now occupy the site of William
Hazeldine's Plas Kynaston Ironworks where the iron
trough of the Pont Cysyllte aqueduct was cast. Somewhat naturally the conservators decided that if anybody
sold water to this large chemical plant it should be
themselves, and they forthwith successfully challenged
the railway company in the courts. As a result of this
legal action, the canal intake was limited to a stipulated
quantity per day; and to ensure that this was not
exceeded, the railway company were to install a flow
meter at Llantisilio. At the time we made this first
voyage, this flow meter and the house which contained
it were still under construction, and in the meantime
water was being admitted to the canal in extremely
meagre quantities through a temporary by-pass channel.
Yet even if this supply had been more generous, it is

doubtful if it would have helped us very much, for the canal was so choked with weeds that the water would not flow down. Consequently it could be running over the spill weirs at the Llangollen end while at New Martin locks, twelve miles downstream, it could be nine inches low. The Welsh Canal supplies a reservoir at Hurleston which, in turn, supplies the main line of the Shropshire Union between Hack Green, Chester and Ellesmere Port. So it was not only the Welsh Canal which suffered from this parlous water situation.

We awoke next morning to find that the water level in the canal had risen slightly and we were able to struggle on as far as the repaired drawbridge at Wrenbury. Here there was a turning place or 'winding hole' where, despite its disused and depressing appearance, we reckoned we might be able to turn *Cressy*. I have never been one who throws in the sponge lightly, so it is a measure of the appalling state of the canal that we seriously considered making a strategic retreat to Hurleston. Before making a final decision, however, I lifted down Angela's bicycle from the deck and cycled along the towpath to see what conditions were like ahead. There appeared to be more water and less weed so we decided to forge on.

Soon bow-hauling was no longer necessary, but a rising cross wind made progress increasingly difficult for *Cressy*, and at teatime we decided to moor up for the night above Marbury Lock, leaving *Heron* to go ahead as the Grundys were anxious to ascend the lock flight at Grindley Brook before nightfall.

We eventually reached Grindley Brook only to find

that *Cressy* again stuck fast between the wing walls of the bottom lock. It was only after repeated 'flushing' from the top paddles that eventually, to our great relief, she came free and we were able to tie up to the bank below the lock. Here we held a council of war. Somehow or other we had to get *Cressy* up the Grindley Brook flight, for the prospect of retreat now did not bear thinking about; it would have meant stern-hauling our heavy boat back to that 'winding hole' at Wrenbury, and even there it was by no means certain that we could turn her. The day was Sunday, and we walked up to the lock house at the top of the flight where we explained our predicament to the lock keeper, Mr Howell, who promised to come down with an assistant to give us a hand next morning.

I spent most of the rest of the day planing obvious high spots off *Cressy*'s wooden hull. I also greased her bow rubbing strakes, for I had resolved upon the desperate expedient of driving her at full speed towards the lock chamber. If she went in, well and good; if she did not, I realized that nothing would free her short of partly demolishing a lock wall as Brunel and Claxton had had to do in order to get the *Great Britain* out of Bristol Docks. There was another snag to this scheme: to be quite certain that she was well and truly in the lock chamber, I would have to keep her going full ahead so long that it would be extremely difficult to prevent her cannoning violently into the top gate sill. Such a disaster could only be averted if Angela checked her at the right moment with a 'stern strap' and at the same instant all the top gate paddles were raised.

When Mr Howell and his mate appeared next morning I explained my plan to him and, though he looked extremely dubious, as well he might, he agreed that it was the only thing to do under the circumstances. So, having secured everything on board that might be damaged by a possible impact, we moved *Cressy* astern for fifty yards or so and then, with a silent prayer, I gave her full ahead and approached the narrow chamber at what appeared to be an impossible speed. Everything worked perfectly. There was a creaking sound and I felt her check slightly as the side walls nipped her, but the next moment she was through. Angela had checked her with the stern line, Mr Howell had raised the top paddles, and a few seconds later the lower gates had slammed to behind me with a crash. I felt *Cressy* surge upwards. So far so good, but there were still five more locks to go, culminating in a triple lock staircase of awesome depth. It was so many years since a narrow boat had passed through the canal that Mr Howell was as much in the dark as we were as to the likely outcome of our venture. In the event, *Cressy* stuck again firmly coming out of the third lock and I had to use our pulley blocks to free her; yet, curiously enough, although the lock keeper had dire misgivings about the state of the staircase, she came through it without the slightest difficulty. It was with immense relief that we moored opposite Mr Howell's cottage at the top of the flight and caught a bus into Whitchurch to do our weekly shopping.

One could see from the weir beside the top lock that the canal level was at least six inches below normal; and in order to keep the lower part of the canal and Hurleston reservoir supplied, Mr Howell had the special by-pass paddle drawn. A very long level now lay ahead of us, so we could not expect any improvement but must make the best of it. As soon as we started off, it was obvious that the bottom was much too near the top. Happily, however, there was little or no weed and we were able to make slow but steady progress under our own power for a mile or two until we reached a point which, according to that canal traveller's bible, de Salis's *Guide*, was known as Blackoe Cottages. Here *Cressy* ran suddenly and firmly aground in mid-channel; so firmly, in fact, that her bows rose up out of the water. Investigation soon showed that a small stream flowed into the canal at this point and that over the years it had built up a bar of silt that extended from bank to bank.

Once again my pulley blocks and extra lines proved invaluable. Just above the mouth of the brook grew a stout tree whose bole made an ideal anchor for my double block, the single block being hooked on to *Cressy*'s fore-end stud. Then the free end of the cotton line was taken across the canal to the towpath where a long pull and a strong pull by Angela and myself, assisted by most of the astonished inhabitants of Blackoe Cottages, was sufficient to drive *Cressy* through the silt barrier. We then had lunch before continuing slowly on our way as far as the old wharf and bridge at Platt Lane where we found a party of gypsies encamped in a green road and stopped for a cup of tea to satisfy a mutual curiosity.

It was over this same Welsh canal that I had made my first voyage by inland waterway in 1930 at a time when

Cressy was steam driven. The canal had seemed to me then to be so uniquely and magically beautiful that I was at once captivated by the idea of travelling by waterway. This narrow and winding ribbon of water conveyed such a strange sense of remoteness and seemed to pass through such an astonishing variety of scenery. Now, returning to the same canal in the same boat after the lapse of seventeen years, I was interested to discover whether my first impressions had been correct, or whether I had been beguiled by distance and nostalgia. I could still recall vividly the enchantment of that first voyage, gliding through the glassy waters on that spring morning so long ago. I recalled ruefully that it had then been easy going and not a perpetual struggle with weed, lack of water and decaying lock chambers. Yet despite all the effort and anxiety, I decided as we left Platt Lane that it was worth it; the magic remained; it was no illusion.

At Platt Lane the Welsh Canal undergoes its first dramatic transformation. Up to this point we had been travelling through a typical Cheshire countryside of gently rolling pastures and large dairy farms of blackish red brick; a pleasant enough scene but somewhat tame. Now we suddenly found ourselves in a landscape that reminded us of our last year's journey across the great Bog of Allen on the Grand Canal of Ireland. Whixall Moss is indeed a replica of an Irish turf bog set down on the Shropshire/Cheshire borders, and the Welsh Canal cuts straight across it. For some reason, presumably connected with the nature of the peat, the canal becomes not only weed-free but both wider and deeper as soon as it enters upon the bog, so that from crawling along at snail's pace *Cressy* was suddenly able to travel as fast as upon some broad river. They had been cutting turf on the Moss, and the dark stacks of drying peats in the middle distance backed by the distant shapes of the Berwyns beyond, serenely blue and indistinct in the haze of the summer's day, made the resemblance to an Irish landscape complete.

We reached the end of Whixall Moss all too soon and once again the canal became narrow, shallow and winding, its banks lined with the yellow flowers of musk. But we were now in the wilder border country, quite unlike the broad pastures of Cheshire. Presently we reached the little village of Bettisfield where we decided to moor for the night. Politically, *Cressy* had now entered Wales for the first time since 1930, for Bettisfield is in 'Flintshire detached', that strange little Welsh island in Shropshire. Physically, however, those distant blue mountains marked the true Welsh border whither we were bound – or so I hoped.

After dinner that evening we strolled down the road into the village and had a drink at the 'Nag's Head'. The first thing I noticed as we entered the small tap room was a broken luggage rack bracket out of a railway coach reposing in a glass case on the wall. I had encountered some queer objects in pubs in my time, but nothing as odd as this. On inquiry, it transpired that this was a relic of the Welshampton railway disaster which took place on the main line of the old Cambrian Railway that runs parallel with the canal at this point. Apart from the better known – and worse – accident at Abermule,

Welshampton was the only serious disaster that the Cambrian suffered.

A little distance beyond Bettisfield, the Welsh Canal springs a second surprise, comparable in beauty to Whixall Moss though of an entirely different character. It passes through the heart of what is sometimes called the Shropshire Lake District, a number of shallow, tree-fringed meres in the neighbourhood of the little town of Ellesmere. The water of these meres normally appears dark and peaty, especially under the shade of the encircling trees, but once a year a brief phenomenon, known locally as the 'break', occurs when a species of algae rises to the surface to turn the water an opaque green. Ellesmere itself, the largest of these meres, is also the most open and the most frequented, being the nearest to the town. By contrast, Colemere (pronounced 'Coomer' by the locals) and Blake Mere are tree-surrounded and secluded, the haunt of many wild-fowl. The canal passes close beside them and I remembered the impression they had made upon me when I had first seen them from *Cressy*'s deck in the grey stillness of an early spring dawn. Now under the clear light of the summer sun I found they had lost nothing of their earlier enchantment. We moored up under the shade of the trees beside the narrow bank that divides the canal from Colemere and had a very protracted picnic lunch, interrupted only by the intermittent clucking and splashing of the coot and moorhen which alone flawed the mirror of the water. We felt it was a fitting reward for all the effort and anxieties involved in forcing a passage through waters which, in the course of recent years, had become virtually uncharted. Yet how many times, I reflected, must *Cressy* have passed this way in the course of her working life when she was one of the Shropshire Union Canal Carrying Company's fleet or, later, when she belonged to the owners of a mill at Maesbury.

Although the going had been slow since we left Whixall Moss, the canal had been pleasantly free from weed; but after lunch, as we passed through the very short Ellesmere tunnel, we saw that the canal ahead was choked with a dense blanket of green. So thick was it that it was only with the help of bow-hauling from the towpath that we covered the brief remaining distance to the junction of the short Ellesmere branch canal. At this point, the main line of canal curves sharply southward, rounding Beech House, once the headquarters of the old Ellesmere Canal Company, and the extensive canal workshops. As at Wrenbury, we decided once again that discretion was the better part of valour and that it would be better to explore what lay ahead on foot before passing so convenient a turning point for *Cressy*. What we saw ahead could scarcely have been more discouraging; the canal was choked with dense weed as far as the eye could see. Moreover, we were told at the canal workshops that this state of things prevailed at least as far as New Marton locks and that even if we fought our way through this Sargasso Sea of weed, we could go no further than Chirk because a slip in the deep cutting to the north of Chirk tunnel had made the canal quite impassable.

So, once again, despite all our efforts, my ambition to take *Cressy* over Pont Cysyllte had been defeated; the way into Wales was closed to us, and it then seemed most unlikely that it would ever reopen. Sadly, we swung *Cressy* about in the mouth of the junction and tied her up alongside the towpath by Beech House. Although this was convenient for the town it was by no means ideal in other respects; so, as we had planned to stay in the area for several summer weeks, we determined to retrace our steps for three and a half miles to a disused wharf at Hampton Bank which had looked both inviting and convenient when we had passed it by.

Hampton Bank Wharf did indeed prove to be an almost ideal mooring. It lay just off the road from Ellesmere to Wem which then carried little traffic and from which the wharf was readily accessible. Although the wharf was grass-grown it provided a good hard standing for a car. A solitary cottage – obviously built for a wharfinger – was still occupied by a kindly country couple who gladly supplied us with drinking water and kept an eye on the boat when we were away. Here I left Angela in charge of *Cressy* while I travelled by train to Banbury for the purpose of collecting my Alvis.

During these summer weeks at Hampton Bank, despite having the Alvis, we made good use of the local railway system – in this case part of what had once been the old Cambrian Railway – for the sheer pleasure of sampling rural branch lines. It was a hobby which combined well with living afloat. We used that part of the Cambrian main line which keeps the canal company most of the way between Whitchurch, Ellesmere and Oswestry. We also travelled to Wrexham by the branch line from Ellesmere and, best of all, trundled up the

Tanat Valley branch from Oswestry to Llanrhaiadr y Mochnant in a diminutive train of Cambrian four-wheelers, now smartly painted in G.W.R. livery; it was drawn by a little tank engine, the *Lady Margaret*, which had originally seen service on the Liskeard & Looe Railway in faraway Cornwall but had now come north to work out her last days in this remote Welsh valley.

From mid-July to mid-August, while *Cressy* lay at Hampton Bank, the weather was exceptionally fine and warm. Pleasant though it was, this four-week spell of heat and unbroken drought began to affect the canal. At first it was only a matter of an inch or two, but then the level suddenly began to fall alarmingly. Inquiries elicited the gloomy information that there had been a burst in the canal bank in the neighbourhood of Chirk and that in consequence the temporary feed from the Dee at Llantisilio had been shut off pending repairs. We had entered this abandoned canal at our own risk and peril and had no rights whatever; *Cressy* could sit on the mud at Hampton Bank until doomsday for all the L.M.S. railway cared, so it was up to us to do something quickly. For a while, business was brisk in the telephone kiosk at Hampton Bank. It was obvious that so long as Mr Howell, the lock keeper at Grindley Brook, continued to draw water down through his by-pass culvert into the canal below the locks, the situation would worsen rapidly. On the telephone he sounded most anxious to help, but said he dared not shut off supplies to Hurleston reservoir without authority from Crewe. So, in response to an S.O.S. message to Crewe, a remote official in the L.M.S. finally agreed somewhat grudgingly that Howell could drop his by-pass paddle for twenty-four hours and no longer. All this took place on a Sunday (17 August), and by the time we had got confirmation from Howell that he had complied with instructions it was 6 p.m. We got under way without more ado, travelling in close company with *Heron*. We were dragging the bottom as far as Bettisfield, but after this the going improved somewhat and by 9 p.m. we had reached Platt Lane Wharf, where we decided to lie for the night.

Remembering our experience on the upward journey, it was obvious that the toughest part of this race against the clock was still to come, but fortunately help was at hand in the person of one of the early members of the I.W.A. and his wife. He was a sterling character named Livock, an ex-R.A.F. Squadron Leader who, before the war, had pioneered the flying-boat route to Singapore. Precisely how we got in touch with each other at this providential moment I cannot now remember and my log is silent on the subject. Suffice it to say that Livock and his wife drove on to Platt Lane Wharf in a large estate car promptly at 9 a.m. the next morning. We then proceeded to discharge from *Cressy*'s aft hold everything that could be spared – five gallon drums of spare fuel, off-cuts of locomotive frame-plates from Kerr Stuart which had been serving as ballast ever since those far-off days at Stoke-on-Trent when *Cressy* had been steam-driven. All this was loaded into the back of the estate car. It settled down on its back springs rather like a broody hen, but at the same time *Cressy*'s stern rose out of the water nearly two inches. At a time when every inch counted, this was probably crucial. The transfer completed, Mrs Livock then set off in the car with instructions to keep in touch so far as possible until – we hoped – we were able to switch cargoes again at Basin End, Nantwich. Her husband remained with us to supply the extra muscle power which we would certainly need. *Cressy* then set off, towing *Heron* astern and with Angela, Livock and Christopher Grundy bow-hauling from the towpath. Their efforts were only occasionally needed until we reached Blackoe Cottages where, remembering the trouble we had previously had with the shoal across the canal, I thought we would most probably meet our Waterloo. Once more I rigged our blocks and tackle, but this time it was a much tougher proposition. For a long time, strain as we would, *Cressy* refused to budge until finally a team of nine, the combined crews of both boats, plus Livock, plus three able-bodied recruits from the Cottages, were mustered together on the towpath. Digging in our heels and heaving like a tug-o'-war team, we suddenly felt the line give in our hands and, with mutual cries of encouragement, we fought our way backward foot by foot as we watched *Cressy* drive partly through and partly over the obstruction. It was an immense relief to see her floating once more and on the 'home' side of the barrier. We celebrated victory by calling a brief halt for a lunch that consisted mainly of very welcome liquor.

Lack of water had worsened the weed problem, and when we continued after lunch we several times had to resort to bow-hauling for this reason. But now that our main concern was to stay afloat, weeds seemed a relatively minor worry. So, partly under power and partly bow-hauled, our boats arrived at Grindley Brook, with a very tired and sweaty crew in attendance, at 4 p.m. or just two hours inside our twenty-four-hour time limit. Mr Howell was delighted to see us. He had expected to see *Heron* but confessed that he had had grave doubts whether *Cressy* would be able to make it. Now, with her bows nudging the top gate of the triple staircase lock while we brewed a cup of tea, I no longer had any fear that we might be stranded. Once on the other side of that gate, there was no doubt at all in my mind that Mr Howell would let down enough water to float us back to Hurleston even if it meant emptying the entire upper portion of the canal. And so it proved. Looking down, we could see that the short pound between the bottom of the staircase and Lock No. 16 was completely dry, and both our boats had to lie in the chambers of the staircase while water was passed down to fill it. The bottom lock at Grindley Brook, where we had stuck so fast on the upward journey, did not delay us this time. With all the top paddles up and her engine going full ahead, *Cressy* shot out of that lock chamber like a cork from a champagne bottle. But not far, for the canal below the flight looked so low that we decided to tie up for the night to allow the pound to make up. After all, we were no longer working to a deadline and time was now on our side.

Our progress next day was very slow but sure, for now we were literally bringing with us the precious water we needed. This meant that there had to be lengthy pauses at each lock while we ran the water down from the pound above to the pound below. Apart from this there is little to say about the last stage of our adventurous foray up the Welsh Section. We spent the next night at the head of Baddiley top lock, and at 6 p.m. on the evening of the day following we moored in Nantwich Basin where we were able to relieve Mrs Livock of her car load of fuel and ballast. We celebrated victory that night with a protracted and memorable dinner at the 'Crown Hotel' in Nantwich. Everyone was in high good humour, for there is nothing to equal the power of an episode of this kind as a generator of friendship and fellow-feeling.

Next day we parted company, *Heron* sailing north towards Chester, while *Cressy* swung her bows southward. Our destination was Gayton Arm End, where the Northampton Branch of the Grand Union Canal joins the main line of that canal near Blisworth. We travelled via the Staffordshire & Worcestershire and the Trent & Mersey canals, and the rivers Trent and Soar to Leicester, where we joined the Leicester Section of the Grand Union. This whole journey of 203 miles from Hampton Bank Wharf on the Welsh Marches to Northamptonshire took sixteen days and I recorded the fact that throughout this time we enjoyed unbroken sunshine.

There was a particular reason why we had made Gayton and not Banbury our immediate objective. During our stay at Hampton Bank I had been pondering over possible ways of attracting new members to our Association and publicizing its canal crusade, and had hit on the notion of staging a canal exhibition in London. The great question was *where*, for the infant I.W.A. certainly could not afford to hire any gallery in central London. Then I thought of Anthony Heal whom I had

known since the earliest days of the Vintage Sports
Car Club at the Phoenix. Anthony received my idea
enthusiastically, and readily agreed that we might use
the Mansard Gallery outside the restaurant on the top
floor of the Heal family's famous shop in Tottenham
Court Road. With this satisfactorily settled it became a
question of collecting suitable material for exhibition,
and we had agreed that Gayton was the most convenient
base from which to pursue this quest. Not only was it
conveniently near the main line to Euston, but the Grand
Union carried a much larger floating population than did
the Oxford Canal. There was a third reason also. At
Gayton Junction were situated the canal workshops for
the district, and the home and offices of the district
engineer, C. N. Hadlow. Charles Hadlow was a friend
of mine and a canal engineer of wide experience with a
deep interest in the canal past. So much so that, on his
retirement, he played a great part in the setting up of the
present Waterways Museum at Stoke Bruerne of which
he became honorary curator. I guessed – rightly as things
turned out – that he would be the best person to assist
us in locating suitable material for display. It so happened
that he had lately discovered, in an old loft over one of
the canal buildings at Gayton, a pile of old glass-plate
negatives, all showing early canal scenes, which had been
taken by his predecessors. To examine this treasure-trove
in his office, holding them up to the light and deciding
which ones to print up, was a fascinating exercise.
Charles Hadlow was able to lend us a pair of the brass
armlets which were issued by the old Grand Junction
Canal Company to the professional 'leggers' who had

once been responsible for propelling the boats through Blisworth tunnel at 1s. 6d. a time. This was only one of the many two- and three-dimensional objects – boat furniture, traditional boaters' clothing, model boats, some made by professionals and others by the boatmen themselves – which we managed to collect in a surprisingly short space of time, for we had arrived at Gayton on 4 September and the Exhibition was due to open on 25 October. The find which most pleased me was a splendid diorama showing a pair of horse-drawn narrow boats entering the top lock at Stoke Bruerne. I cannot remember how we got to know of the existence of this, but I remember collecting it from its owner's garage in the suburbs of Leighton Buzzard. He explained that, with other dioramas, it had been made by his father many years before.

Angela and I spent several days arranging all this material in Heals' Mansard Gallery, an unfamiliar and satisfying task which we thoroughly enjoyed and which we were able to complete on time despite frequent interruptions. We walked in fear of one formidable lady of middle age who was in charge of the gallery and very evidently disapproved of our amateurish goings-on. She seemed to lurk perpetually in a little office in a corner of the gallery from which she would dart out at us from time to time whenever she observed us in the act of committing some dire offence such as sticking drawing pins into the woodwork. Altogether more encouraging and enjoyable were the visits of Anthony's father, old Sir Ambrose Heal, who took a lively and intelligent interest in our enterprise.

This 'Inland Waterways Exhibition' proved a great success. It attracted so much attention from press and public that I succeeded in persuading some commercial firm (I forget the name) to pack up the exhibition when it closed at Heals after a month and take it on a tour of provincial art galleries at no cost to the Association. One tragi-comic result of this was that the firm's packers, who were experts at this class of work, discovered that our precious Stoke Bruerne diorama was riddled with woodworm. The discovery that someone was suffering from bubonic plague could scarely have created a greater furore. The unfortunate model was at once isolated and subjected to such a barrage of poisonous sprays that it finally disintegrated and was never heard of again so far as I can remember. Its owner took its loss philosophically since it was obvious that it had become infested during its long years of neglect in his garage. At least his father's patient craftsmanship had enjoyed one final blaze of glory.

THE STORY OF PENGUIN CLASSICS

Before 1946 ...'Classics' are mainly the domain of academics and students, without readable editions for everyone else. This all changes when a little-known classicist, E. V. Rieu, presents Penguin founder Allen Lane with the translation of Homer's Odyssey that he has been working on and reading to his wife Nelly in his spare time.

1946 The Odyssey becomes the first Penguin Classic published, and promptly sells three million copies. Suddenly, classic books are no longer for the privileged few.

1950s Rieu, now series editor, turns to professional writers for the best modern, readable translations, including Dorothy L. Sayers's *Inferno* and Robert Graves's *The Twelve Caesars*, which revives the salacious original.

1960s 1961 sees the arrival of the Penguin Modern Classics, showcasing the best twentieth-century writers from around the world. Rieu retires in 1964, hailing the Penguin Classics list as 'the greatest educative force of the 20th century'.

1970s A new generation of translators arrives to swell the Penguin Classics ranks, and the list grows to encompass more philosophy, religion, science, history and politics.

1980s The Penguin American Library joins the Classics stable, with titles such as *The Last of the Mohicans* safeguarded. Penguin Classics now offers the most comprehensive library of world literature available.

1990s Penguin Popular Classics are launched, offering readers budget editions of the greatest works of literature. Penguin Audiobooks brings the classics to a listening audience for the first time, and in 1999 the launch of the Penguin Classics website takes them online to an ever larger global readership.

The 21st Century Penguin Classics are rejacketed for the first time in nearly twenty years. This world famous series now consists of more than 1,300 titles, making the widest range of the best books ever written available to millions – and constantly redefining the meaning of what makes a 'classic'.

The Odyssey continues ...

The best books ever written

PENGUIN 🐧 CLASSICS

SINCE 1946